Front Street

by

Anne Pié

FOUNDED 1830

NEW YORK HOLLYWOOD LONDON TORONTO

SAMUELFRENCH.COM

Copyright © 1982, 2008 by Anne Pié

ALL RIGHTS RESERVED

CAUTION: Professionals and amateurs are hereby warned that *FRONT STREET* is subject to a royalty. It is fully protected under the copyright laws of the United States of America, the British Commonwealth, including Canada, and all other countries of the Copyright Union. All rights, including professional, amateur, motion picture, recitation, lecturing, public reading, radio broadcasting, television and the rights of translation into foreign languages are strictly reserved. In its present form the play is dedicated to the reading public only.

The amateur live stage performance rights to *FRONT STREET* are controlled exclusively by Samuel French, Inc., and royalty arrangements and licenses must be secured well in advance of presentation. PLEASE NOTE that amateur royalty fees are set upon application in accordance with your producing circumstances. When applying for a royalty quotation and license please give us the number of performances intended, dates of production, your seating capacity and admission fee. Royalties are payable one week before the opening performance of the play to Samuel French, Inc., at 45 W. 25th Street, New York, NY 10010.

Royalty of the required amount must be paid whether the play is presented for charity or gain and whether or not admission is charged.

Stock royalty quoted upon application to Samuel French, Inc.

For all other rights than those stipulated above, apply to: Samuel French, Inc., at 45 W. 25th Street, New York, NY 10010.

Particular emphasis is laid on the question of amateur or professional readings, permission and terms for which must be secured in writing from Samuel French, Inc.

Copying from this book in whole or in part is strictly forbidden by law, and the right of performance is not transferable.

Whenever the play is produced the following notice must appear on all programs, printing and advertising for the play: "Produced by special arrangement with Samuel French, Inc."

Due authorship credit must be given on all programs, printing and advertising for the play.

ISBN 978-0-573-66260-7

No one shall commit or authorize any act or omission by which the copyright of, or the right to copyright, this play may be impaired.

No one shall make any changes in this play for the purpose of production.

Publication of this play does not imply availability for performance. Both amateurs and professionals considering a production are strongly advised in their own interests to apply to Samuel French, Inc., for written permission before starting rehearsals, advertising, or booking a theatre.

No part of this book may be reproduced, stored in a retrieval system, or transmitted in any form, by any means, now known or yet to be invented, including mechanical, electronic, photocopying, recording, videotaping, or otherwise, without the prior written permission of the publisher.

IMPORTANT BILLING AND CREDIT REQUIREMENTS

All producers of *FRONT STREET* must give credit to the Author of the Play in all programs distributed in connection with performances of the Play, and in all instances in which the title of the Play appears for the purposes of advertising, publicizing or otherwise exploiting the Play and/or a production. The name of the Author must appear on a separate line on which no other name appears, immediately following the title and must appear in size of type not less than fifty percent of the size of the title type.

FRONT STREET was given its West Coast premier by CRC Entertainment on March 23, 1996 at St. Genesius Theater in West Hollywood, CA. The production was directed by T. J. Castronovo and was produced by Michael J. Carazza and T. J. Castronovo. The cast, crew and design team were as follows:

CAST:

Mary Tahmin
John Lamotta
Ray Abruzzo
Peter Cerenzio
Katharyn Grant
Robert Forster
Carol Adele Davis
Angelo Vacco
Joey Gaynor
D. V. Caitlyn

SET & LIGHTING DESIGN - David Carleen
WARDROBE DESIGN - Ivana Bailey
WARDROBE DRESSER - Angie Buemi
SOUND TECH - Albert Romano
STAGE MANAGER - Glenn Hendricks
ASSISTANT STAGE MANAGER - Sharon Michelle Lake

VOICEOVERS

DISC JOCKEY, RADIO ANNOUNCER, NEWSCASTER - Larry McCann
CIRCUS ANNOUNCER - Billy Capizzi

THE CAST

NICKY DELUNA - Can be age 10 or 12; dressed in shorts and t-shirt; barefoot.

ANGIE DELUNA - Pretty and fresh looking. She wears summery peasant blouses and skirts. She is seventeen.

TONIA DELUNA - Over forty; wears simple cotton dresses and bib-type aprons. Tired looking, but she still has her good looks.

SONNY DELUNA - In his early twenties; wears factory type clothing; walks with a limp.

NINO - Mafiosa type. Can be any age. Menacing; slickly dressed.

DOMINIC DELUNA - Stoop shouldered; looks unwell. He wears underwear top at home; trousers with suspenders. He is years older than Tonia.

ROCCO DELGROSSO - Wears grey shirt and black pants of a bus driver's uniform. Pleasant looking; he is Tonia's age.

MARIA LABRUTTA - Wears good clothing; brightly colored. Her make up is well-applied. She wears high heels and tasteful costume jewelry. Her hair do is a high pompadour coiled around a rat at the nape of her neck. She wears one white glove with six fingers and carries the other. She is Tonia's age. She is not a caricature.

VICTOR FRANKELINA - He is eighteen, and fresh out of basic training. He wears an Army uniform with the rank of Private.

THE SUITOR - Short and dark, with slicked back hair. His suit is ill fitting. His shoes are run down, and he wears white socks. His neck tie is too short and stained. He can be from late thirties to early fifties.

SETTING

Act One
Scene I - July 5, 1944, Supper time

Scene II - An hour later

Act Two
Scene I - The same evening, several hours later

Scene II - The next afternoon, July 6, 1994

Scene III - Several hours later

Scene IV - An hour later

Scene V - Four days later

PLACE

Hartford, Connecticut
Action takes place in one 24 hour period

AUTHOR'S NOTE

On July 6, 1944, men, women, and children lost their lives in the Ringling Brother Barnum-and-Bailey Circus fire on the Barbour Street fairgrounds in the north end of Hartford. Because the canvas had been waterproofed with a mixture of paraffin and gasoline, flames that began as a fire the size of a baseball spread instantly. The fire raced up the walls and totally engulfed the roof in seconds, which collapsed on everyone below. When the fire was finally extinguished, out of the several thousand people who were under the big top that steamy July day, 168 people had perished and 487 were injured.

A special thanks to T. Castronovo and Michael Carazza for believing in this play and the others that have followed.

ACT ONE

Scene I

Before the lights come up, we hear the radio playing the tag end of "Sentimental Journey" sung by Doris Day.

When the lights are up full, the song ends. Nicky, on the telephone, can be heard over the radio. He holds the receiver with one hand while making circular scrubbing motions on the rocking chair with a long, wooden-handled bowl brush with the other. Nicky's notebook is on the kitchen table, where a coffee cup sits, center, waiting. The coffee pot is on the stove with its contents already heated.

Although it is a hot summer day, the fan which sits on top of the refrigerator is not operating.

NICKY. What? I don't believe you. You got to be kidding. You're making that up, Malucci!

(He sets the brush down)

RADIO ANNOUNCER. You have just been listening to "Sentimental Journey" by Les Brown and His Band of Renown, with the vocal done by the one, the only... Miss Doris Day.

(While still holding the phone, Nicky begins crossing to the radio.)

ANNOUNCER. All the best in radio from WTIC, Hartford, the insurance capital of the world. Now... stayed tuned for this message.

(Circus music begins. Nicky turns the radio off and moves downstage)

NICKY. Oh, yeah!? I do *so* know!

(Down front)

God plants a seed in the mother's belly, and then the baby grows.

Huh? A year, I think.

(He listens)

All right… nine months, then. What's so funny?

That's not the way it is! My Nonie* told me that the mother rubs her belly with olive oil and when the baby is ready, it pops out of her belly button.

(He listens)

No, but I suppose *you* know how it gets there!

(In utter shock)

Geez… you are such a **LIAR,** John Malucci! My father never did that in his whole life. You're going to have to tell that in confession, and I'll bet Father Guidone* gives you a hundred Acts of Contrition!

(Without malice)

Hah… you're the bird-brain.

Malooch, you still coming over tonight? We can listen to "Henry Aldrich" on the radio. Yeah, I gotta go, too. See you later. *(He hangs up)*

(Angie enters hurriedly, carrying a shoe box tied with string.)

NICKY. Gee, Angie. What took you so long?

ANGIE. Nonie left her shoes at the store and I had to go all the way back.

(She calls)

Nonie!

NICKY. She's not home.

ANGIE. But I left her on the porch not half an hour ago.

NICKY. Oh, she's probably across the street having coffee with Gooma' Regina.

---

* No-nie, with long "o"
* Gwe-'don, long "o"; no "e" on end

ANGIE. Of course. Nonie and her coffee. *(Looks at clock on shelf)*

Look at the time... I'm so late.

(She hurries to the mirror beside the kitchen door and scrutinizes herself)

NICKY. *(Worried)* Hey, Ang? Malucci says that coffee's bad for you and will give you the heebie-jeebies if you drink too much. But Nonie says it relaxes her.

(Angie is pre-occupied)

She got up at four o'clock the other morning to make a cup so she could go back to sleep. Malucci says that means she's crazy.

ANGIE. When are you going to stop listening to what that *John Malucci* says?

(Pinches her cheeks for color and runs her fingers through her hair approvingly, patting it into place. Picks up her purse and begins to exit)

Nick, if someone by the name of Victor calls, tell him I'm on my way and to pick a good table.

NICKY. Who's Victor?

ANGIE. See how shiny my hair looks from the rainwater you got for me out of the barrel? How do I look?

NICKY. Okay for a girl. Who's *Victor?*

ANGIE. Just *someone.* I have to run. See you later

(Calls over her shoulder as she exits)

Ma will be home soon. Get her coffee ready.

NICKY. I always have it ready, don't I?

(Crosses to door and shouts after her)

Hey, Ang! I wasn't going to tell you this, but there were big, fat **bugs** in your rainwater.

(Chuckles with satisfaction when he hears her screech. Nicky turns his attention back to the room. He turns on the radio. There is some static before the circus announcement and circus music.)

CIRCUS BARKER. CHILDREN OF A-L-L AGES!

(Nicky crosses to the cushion. While he listens to the announcement, he feels the wet spot, sniffs at it and grimaces. He replaces the cushion, upside-down)

The Ringling-Brothers, Barnum and Bailey Circus brings you the greatest performance in the history of the Greatest Show on Earth!

(Nicky shows excitement at the announcement. He crosses to cookie jar and removes an Italian biscotti. He nibbles on it while he listens, and while he checks the coffee pot)

CIRCUS BARKER. Two days only! Wednesday, July 5th and Thursday, July 6th, on the Barbour Street fairgrounds!

(Getting Tonia's coffee ready is a daily ritual, and Nicky waits with great anticipation. He re-adjusts Tonia's favorite cup to just the right position)

CIRCUS BARKER *(con't)* See the clowns! See the elephants! Mr. and Mrs. Gar-gan-tua! The Flying Walendas with their breath-taking, death-defying aerial phenomena!

(Circus music)

For a day in your life you will never forget…
SEE YOU UNDER THE BIG TOP!

RADIO ANNOUNCER. A news update: Admiral Chester W. Nimitz announced in a communique today, U.S. planes sank five Japanese subs in a raid on Iwo Jima. Complete details at five.

(Music segues into regular programming. As soon as Nicky hears Tonia's footsteps on the porch, he turns off the radio. He hurries to the stove to get the coffee pot, picks it up with a potholder and carries it to the table and pours the coffee.)

(Tonia enters. She sets her purse on the counter. Her empty thermos protrudes)

TONIA. Eh. You.

NICKY. Hi, Ma.

(The biscotti is still in his mouth)

TONIA. Mio, caro. You are my dolly boy. No one makes Mamma's coffee like you.

(She pulls him to her, removes the cookie from his mouth, and plants a kiss on his face and returns the cookie to his mouth.)

(Nicky return pot to stove)

TONIA. *(Sits in the chair and rubs her knees)* Ah-h. It feels so good to sit down. You gotta stand up all day, and that goddam shed is like fire by three o'clock.

NICKY. They should let you come home.

TONIA. They don't let you come home. You gotta die first.

NICKY. Then why don't you stay home and let *me* work on tobacco? I'm big enough to pick leaves.

TONIA. Oh, no... you're too young. Besides, you think it's easy to crawl on your hands and knees in the dirt all day in the hot sun under that net?

NICKY. But Sonny picked leaves... with his bad foot... and everything.

TONIA. Eh... Sonny!

(Crosses to sink and deposits cup)

Sonny quit the school. He didn't know how to do anything else.

(Over her shoulder)

You think he'd be at the aircraft like he is now if we didn't have this war, God forbid! He'd still be picking tobacco.

NICKY. But if I could earn some money, I could give it to you, like Sonny does.

TONIA. *(Crosses to the refrigerator)* Ma...State zitti*... please!

(Opens the door and takes out paper-wrapped, roll of salami)

Sonny likes to play the cards. Poker, craps... you name... he plays... capeesh? And he throws money

---

* *Stah - Te ZEE - tee (Be quiet)*

away on the numbers. *(Unwraps the salami)*
He's gonna win big, he says. He wins all right!

(She slices the salami with vehemence)

He wins *merda!* And where's the money, now? In the pockets of those bums he hangs around. No! You are never gonna work on tobacco.

(She rewraps the roll)

You are gonna go to school, study the work, and write in the book.
Senti?

(Cross to refrigerator and returns the roll)

And you are not gonna dig ditches like your Papa. He's got no health anymore. Now he's only good to clean the buses at the car barn; when he feels good.

(Hugs Nicky to her)

That is not for my boy. You gonna be the best!

(She takes a dollar bill out of her dress pocket. Crosses to open cupboard shelf and takes down a sugar bowl from top, back of shelf. She removes the lid and takes out a wad of bills, and wraps the new one around it)

See? Every week... so-h. You don't tell anyone.

(Puts her fingers to her lips)

Every single week, I put away one dollar for your college.

(A beat)

My Nicola* Dominic DeLuna is gonna grow up to be somebody.

(Puts lid back on bowl and returns it to the shelf. Tonia leads Nicky to center chair at table gently steers him into it. She stands behind him with her hands on his shoulders.)

When I carried you inside my body, I knew that you were gonna be special.

* *Ni - KOHL - ah*

It was not like with the others. Never one day was I sick with you. And just before you were born… just before the mid-wife came and took you and placed you on my breast… *guess* who came and whispered in my ear!

NICKY. *(Bored with this story he's heard repeatedly, he rolls his eyes upwards and drops his head on his arm.)* Who?

TONIA. St. Anthony!

(Her voice full of awe)

NICKY. You didn't see him, Ma, so how did you know it was St. Anthony?

TONIA. I don't have to see.

NICKY. Yeah?! So what did St. Anthony say?

TONIA. He said: "Antonia Deodata DeLuna, God has given you something special in this child. You better take good care of him or I'll break your ass!"

NICKY. Maybe it was St. Matthew… or St. Mark.

TONIA. Oh, no! It was St. Anthony. I am named for him. He is my patron saint. Not one day goes by that I don't send him my prayers.

(She puts her hands together in prayer)

Sant'Antonio mio… Give me strength. Make me to have your patience. Keep me and my family safe from harm. Keep us close to you and our Immaculate Mother, Maria Virgine. Intercede for me in my hour of death. Through Jesu Christo, Our Lord. Amen.

(She blesses herself. Looks over at Nicky who does nothing)

(She taps him in the side of his head)

Hey!

NICKY. Oh. Amen!

(He quickly blesses himself. Without hesitation he jumps up and pulls at her sleeve)

Ma, guess what? The circus is in town. I heard it on radio and there are posters all up and down Front Street. Do you think I could go? *Please.*

TONIA. I don't know, Nicky. How much it cost?

NICKY. Not much for kids. I'll do the dishes all week and... even weed the tomatoes. They've got clowns and elephants and everything.

TONIA. H-m-m. Let me think. In this family, we got a lotta clowns...

NICKY. Ma!

TONIA. But we don't have any elephants. So after I finish to pay the bills, we'll see.

NICKY. Oh, boy! Wait til I tell Malucci.

TONIA. Eh! I didn't say **yes.** I said *we'll see!*

(The telephone rings)

TONIA. Get the phone.

NICKY. Hello? Hello? Come on... I know someone's there, because I can you breathing!
All right, then. I'm hanging up! *(He hangs up.)*
See that? No one answers. The same thing happened *twice* this morning.

TONIA. Eh... kids on vacation... fooling around.

(She shrugs, then looks at clock on shelf)

Papa? Where is he?

NICKY. Pa's out back watering tomatoes.

TONIA. He feel okay today?

NICKY. I think so. He yelled at me all afternoon.

TONIA. Eh! Papa is not Papa unless he's yelling at someone. Usually me! And Nonie... where's your grandmother? It's time for mangia. Did Angie take her for the new shoes today?

NICKY. Yeah, but Angie had to force her to go. Nonie cried and said she still had plenty of shoes from the old country.

TONIA. She doesn't have plenty. She has so many holes in her shoes she walks on the ground. I was so ashamed when I see that old lady kneel down at the communion rail last Sunday. Everybody in the first two pews laughed liked hell. Even Father Guidone turned around from the altar to see what the hell all the laughing was. Here. Set the table.

(Hands some dishes to Nicky)

Then after mass, Mrs. Pappallardo, she's big, fat... like a pig, she says: "Tonia, I see your mother-in-law could use some new shoes, no?" I say: "Oh, she just forgot to put the new ones today. But inside, I say: "Va fa Napoli, Mrs. Pappallardo."

(She lays silverware around the table)

Look at the time. Where the hell is Sonny?

NICKY. Don't worry, Ma. He only goes to those places when it's dark.

TONIA. Ma Donna! Even the kid sees!

NICKY. Don't be mad.

TONIA. I'm not mad. It's just that Sonny's not the same inside anymore since the his foot got twisted with the polio.

NICKY. Ma... do you think... well... do you think Nonie is going crazy?

(Worried)

TONIA. Who told you that?

NICKY. John Malucci. He says that Nonie is going crazy in the head and they're going to take her away. He saw her in Livecchi's* Bakery... going like this... at one of the customers.

(He demonstrates; makes the sign of the horns)

Everyone laughed at her.

TONIA. Eh..wait John Malucci! Some day he's gonna get old, too. Nonie's got old age, that's all. So she made the sign of the horns. It don't hurt nobody.

(She spots the pillow. Nicky suddenly become engrossed in his book. Tonia turns cushion over and feels wet spot. She is puzzled.)

---

* *Liv - EK - eze*

This cushion is wet. Per che?

(Nicky feigns deeper interest in his book)

I said, this pillow is bagnata*. Why?

(Nicky does not reply)

You spill something?

(She moves toward him)

Nicky?

NICKY. It'll be all right. Just let it dry.

TONIA. All right. I will let it dry. It don't make no difference. It's an old chair.

(A beat)

Nonie did it, si?

(Nicky again feigns reading)

You can tell me. Nonie peed the chair... no?

NICKY. She didn't mean it.

TONIA. She couldn't help it. Sometimes old people have trouble that way.

NICKY. She peed the bed the other night, too.

TONIA. That's nothing. We washed the sheets.

NICKY. John Malucci was here when she peed the chair. He said if she keeps doing that they're going to take her away and lock her up for sure. And this morning, when Angie took her for the shoes, she was all mixed up again. John Malucci says...

TONIA. Eh... shut up with John Malucci... please! I'm sick of John Malucci! That goddam kid thinks he knows tutti cosi!

(She draws Nicky from the couch and holds him)

Nobody is gonna take our Nonie. And if they did, where would they put her? They got no place. In our house, we take care of our own. You remember this thing, Nicky. La famiglia e molta importanta! Even if we yell and fight and scream, we always gotta stick together. Capeesh?

* bahn - YAH - ta (wet)

NICKY. I guess so.

TONIA. And now... let's go wash that face... my dolly-boy-cu-la-facia-sporca*!

(She lovingly takes him by the ear, pulls him up and steers him toward the hall)

NICKY. I washed it yesterday.

(The lights begin to come down)

TONIA. And look at your knees. You gotta 'nuff dirt to grow potatoes!

NICKY. I can do it myself.

TONIA. Come-on, come-on, figlio mio bellissimo!

(The lights continue to fade. Tonia tickles Nicky as they exit)

NICKY. MA! Cut it out!

(The lights are out on the kitchen)

End Act I, Scene I

---

* *coo - la - facha - SPORK- o (with the dirty face)*

Scene II

One hour later.

As the lights come down on Tonia and Nicky's exit, they come up on the entrance to the alley outside the tenement. It can be a simple suggestion of an alley with a trash can and wooden box of assorted discards to one side.

A man leans just inside the alley, waiting. He is well-dressed, smoking a cigarette. When Sonny enters, he drops the cigarette and grinds it out in a menacing manner.

Sonny has a limp. He is wearing coveralls and is carrying a metal lunch box. His eyes downward, he is preoccupied, and he is visibly startled when Nino steps out.

NINO. Hey... guaillio*.

(Sonny jumps back)

What happened? We missed you at the restaurant.

SONNY. Jesus, Nino! Ya tryin' to scare me to death? What are you doing here?

NINO. *(Coldly)* I think you forgot something.

SONNY. *(Lowering his voice, he draws closer)* I would have brought it over tonight.

NINO. Oh, yeah? Hand it over now.

(Holds out his hand)

SONNY. I don't have it here.

(With braggadocio)

Hey! I was gonna change my clothes first and show you my new suit.

NINO. You got too many new suits. And, you welch on your bets, kid.

SONNY. For Chris'sake... what are you talking about? Don't you trust me?

(Nino does not answer)

Ask anyone on the street. I got a reputation. DaLuna

---

* *Guail - lio, pronounced "wall-yo," (fellow)*

pays.

NINO. Sure. You pay. But you pay when you feel like it and you don't pay it all.

SONNY. That's a lie. I don't cheat anyone.

NINO. So. We saw you come in and then leave in an awful hurry. Cappella was a little hurt… you know? He sez to me… he sez… "How do you like that? He didn't even stop by to give a friendly hello." So I sez.."Have a heart, Capella. Maybe Sonny's near-sighted and needs glasses."

(He smiles)

Is that what it was, Sonny? You didn't see us and that's why you didn't come to the booth?

SONNY. Jesus. I couldn't. When I walked in, there was my kid sister sittin' at one of the tables.

NINO. You could've give us a sign.

SONNY. I told you before. I don't want my family involved.

NINO. *(Laughing quietly, he saunters up to Sonny)*

You're funny, kid. You know? You got it kind of backwards. You don't tell us. We tell *you!*

(On "you," he pushes Sonny against the wall and punches him hard in the stomach. When Sonny comes up for air, he slaps him in the face. Sonny reacts more in shock than in pain).

NINO. *(Clutches Sonny's shirt)* Where is it?

SONNY. *(Gasping for air)* In the house.

NINO. Open the box.

SONNY. *(Sonny quickly opens up the lunch box and shows him it's empty.)*

See! Nothin'! I told you.

(Nino slams the lunch box into the trash barrel)

NINO. Get it.

SONNY. I can't. My family is there. I told you before…

(He catches himself. Frightened, he tries to regain his

composure)

Come on, Nino. You know me! I was only keepin' it safe because I collected so much this time.

NINO. If you're lying, I know a little Wop-Ginzo who's gonna have *two* crippled legs!

SONNY. I'm not lyin'. I swear! What's the matter with you?

NINO. One hour.

SONNY. What?

NINO. That's how much time you got. Capeesh?

SONNY. I just got home. I need a little more time than that. There's some things I gotta do.

NINO. *(Suddenly gentle)* Cappella and me, we'll be waitin'. Don't disappoint us. You wouldn't want to hurt Cappella's feelings again.

(He reaches over and pats Sonny's cheek with a sinister tenderness)

(Sonny flinches at Nino's touch)

Huh, kid?

(Begins exit. Snaps his fingers and turns back)

What'sa matter with my brains? I almost forgot to tell you. I don't come to you no more. If I do, be ready. My face will be the last face you see. Ciao!

(Nino exits whistling in a sinister manner)

(The lights begin to come down on Sonny who is full of humiliation, rage and fear. He retrieves the lunch box from the trash barrel, which he re-clasps and tries to wipe off).

(As he limps into the alley, the lights are down, and come up in thekitchen where Nicky is seated at the table, writing in his book.)

(Sonny enters.)

SONNY. *(To Nicky)* Hey, chooch.

(Nervous. Crosses to the mirror and rubs his chin.)

NICKY. Hey, Ma… Sonny's home!

(Tonia enters from the bedroom hall. Nicky returns to his notebook.)

TONIA. What's the matter? What's that mark on your chin?

SONNY. What? This? Oh, I bumped it on the car door.

TONIA. Put some ice.

SONNY. I'm fine.

TONIA. Let me see.

SONNY. *(He shouts at her.)* I said I'm okay!

TONIA. E-h-h-h!

(Shrugs her hurt and exits to dining room.)

NICKY. Gee, Sonny. How come you're late? Ma was worried.

(Sits at table with book)

SONNY. Uh… accident on the bridge coming in from East Hartford.

(Sits on couch; changes the subject.)

Come here, kid.

NICKY. No!

SONNY. I ain't gonna tickle you. I wanna see what you're writing.

NICKY. It's a poem, but it's not finished yet. It still needs fixing.

SONNY. *(Opens book. Reads.)* That's okay. I just wanna sneak preview.

(He scans the material.)

Wow. About a dog, huh?

(Aloud.)

"In the early morning twilight, When the sun burned through the gray…
Asleep beside his master's bed, Shep, a good dog, lay."

(Impressed)

This is pretty good, kid.

NICKY. Really, Sonny?

SONNY. I can almost see his tail wagging.

NICKY. Malucci says writing poetry is dumb… and people make fun of you and say you're a sissy.

SONNY. Number One. For a little kid, that Malucci's got a big mouth. And Number Two, you ain't never been dumb. Got that?

(Creates a drum-roll on the table with his hands)

And now! Ladies and Gentlemen… and especially ole' chooch here…

(With an exaggerated flourish, covers both shirt pockets with his hands)

NICKY. You brought me something?

SONNY. You gotta look for it. Like when you was a little kid.

NICKY. *(Nicky pulls up one hand; empty, he pulls up other hand and finds it)* Wow! An ink pen.

SONNY. If my brother is going to be a famous writer, he's gotta start writin' in ink. No more pencil. That's for amateurs.

NICKY. *(With excitement)* It's beautiful, Sonny. Is it real gold?

SONNY. Sorry to say it ain't. But it will be someday, and I'll lay you odds I'm gonna be the one who buys it for you.

NICKY. I *love* it, Sonny. Thanks.

(Pockets the pen. Sonny crosses to refrigerator.)

SONNY. Hey… nothing's too good for my favorite kid brother! Wanna beer?

NICKY. Aw… cut it out.

SONNY. Well, you're lucky because there's only one left.

(Tonia enters carrying napkins for the table.)

TONIA. What happened, Sonny? It's kind of late. We were worried.

(She removes bowl from refrigerator and sets it on table.

Sonny uncaps the beer and takes a long drink.)

SONNY. Oh, yeah. There… there… was an accident on the bridge from East Hartford.

TONIA. Well, come on. Sit down. Mangia* is ready.
Nicky, go call your PaPa. Tell him supper is ready.

(Nicky exits.)

SONNY. *(Notices fan)* Why don't you put the fan on? It's hot in here.

TONIA. It's broke.

SONNY. Get a new one.

TONIA. Give me the money. I'll get it. Sit and eat.

(She picks up large spoon)

SONNY. It's too hot. I don't wanna eat.

TONIA. I got everything ready.

SONNY. *(Leans over and examines contents of bowl)* Macaroni, again! If it's not with the tomato sauce, you make macaroni salad.

TONIA. Remember, we're Italian in this house. We eat pasta.

SONNY. Yeah, but do we have to have it every day? I mean, I like it, but not every day. How about some meat once in a while?

TONIA. You forget there's a war on, big shot? You bring me the meat… I'll cook it. More better, give the money, I'll find the meat. Even if I don't have the ration stamps.

SONNY. I give you money.

TONIA. When you get a few dollars left over. You don't give it to me regular. But the stomach works regular, doesn't it?

SONNY. Jesus, Ma. You work. Pa works, and now Angie has that part-time job. What do you want from me?

TONIA. Where's your brains! Your father's a sick man. You know we can't count on his money. He only works when he feels good. The only reason they keep him at the car barn is the compare. If he wasn't a cousin of

* *mahn - JA (dinner)*

the boss, PaPa would have no job at all.

SONNY. I'm sorry, Ma. I know Pa's sick. I don't want to start nothin'.

(Rises. Crosses to daybed and flops down)

I'm hot. I'm tired. We've been working a lot of over-time at the plant. I'll try to give you some money next week. All right? Just don't start with me.

TONIA. Next week? What about this week?

SONNY. I got the car payment. I need to get some work done on the car and all of a sudden the radio quit. I probably need a new one.

TONIA. What else? You got the car payment, and you gotta get a radio. You got no house to support... no family... no food to buy. What else?

(She shoves each chair around table to emphasize each item.)

SONNY. I got... responsibilities.

TONIA. You got merda! You owe the bums, like yourself you are getting to be. My God, Sonny. When are you going to listen to me?

SONNY. I'm not gonna listen! I'm gettin' cleaned up and I'm leavin'.

(Sets beer on table)

I don't want no supper. I'll eat at Marilyn's.

(Exits to his bedroom stage left)

TONIA. Eh... Marilyn.

SONNY. *(Back in doorway, he shouts)* What is it, Ma? I get in the house and in five minutes you're all over my back! Just leave me the hell alone for once... okay? I got enough to worry about?

TONIA. How much longer do you think you are going to fool the people, Sonny?

(Sonny exits again)

SONNY. *(off)* About what?

TONIA. Marilyn is *gone*. You think everyone is stupid? She knew if she married you she would end up supporting you for the rest of her life. She was such a nice girl, too. Never missed a day's work at the Traveler's.

SONNY. *(Enters with overalls removed; dressing for evening)* Who needs her!

(Crosses to sink to wash hands)

And what the hell is so good about the Traveler's? It's just another insurance company. You act like it's the goddam White House!

TONIA. It's security, Sonny. Tu capeesh security? I don't know what to tell you anymore.

SONNY. Do me a favor, Ma. Don't tell me nothin'. I don't want to hear it anymore.

(At mirror, tying his tie)

TONIA. *(Crosses to rocker, sits and raises her hem)* Come here. Look at my knees.

SONNY. What is this? What am I supposed to see? They look like normal knees to me.

TONIA. They are not normal. They are swollen.

SONNY. Oh, yeah. From the tobacco sheds. I know.

TONIA. Wrong. They got that way from one whole year being on my knees praying for your goddam vocation.

SONNY. Oh, Ma!

TONIA. One whole year I knelt on that cold, hard floor. Why? Because Sister Avellina said that you had the vocation and that I should bombard heaven with my prayers. So… I bombard. And what do we get? You get the bums, and I get arta-ritis of the knee caps.

SONNY. Who the hell told you to believe that fairy story?

TONIA. Oh. I suppose it was a fairy story that you used to go out in a blizzard at five o'clock in the morning to go to mass? Or that you made the most scapulars for the poor people in Africa, or China, or some goddam country where they always got some kind of shortage?

SONNY. I was a just a kid... for Chris' sake!

TONIA. Eh... so what? You had a gift. You were the best altar boy they ever had at St. Anthony's. When you answered the priest in Latin in that voice so sweet and pure, my breath would catch in my throat.

SONNY. Ma, Sister Avellina wanted me to be a priest. YOU may have wanted me to be a priest, but I never said *I* wanted to be one!

(He shouts)

TONIA. *(Shouting louder)* Lower your voice! How come we can never talk without yelling?

(A beat)

Look, Sonny. Forget about my knees. I probably got twenty or thirty souls out of Purgatory a couple months early. And I don't care if you didn't want to be a priest. But for the love of God, Sonny, be *something!*

SONNY. Well, maybe you don't think I'm something now... but I will be.

TONIA. How? You gonna go back and get the high school diploma? You gonna dump those crooks and start to save your money?

SONNY. No... and NO!

TONIA. That's a good way to start.

SONNY. That way takes too long, Ma. My way is better.

TONIA. Oh. You gotta short cut.

SONNY. Yeah.

TONIA. Ma, che e... this short cut?

SONNY. Che e*? *Money!*

(He enunciates it clearly)

TONIA. Ah-h-h. And... where is this *money?*

(She enunciates it exactly the same way)

SONNY. I don't have it yet. But I will. Soon.

TONIA. Can't you see you are wasting yourself?

SONNY. And can't you see I'm sick of being a second class

---

* *key - a, long "a", (what is)*

citizen. I'm sick of people looking down their nose at me because I'm Italian and live on Front Street! You don't see me eatin' pasta or smellin' of garlic. Never anymore. Ain't no one ever goin' to say to my kid... "Hey, Wop! Your fried pepper sandwich is smellin' up the cloak room. Hey, Wop! I hear the State had to pay for your operation! Hey... you wanna hear a joke? What's worse than bein' a Wop? Bein' a crippled, 4 F Wop!!

TONIA. Oh, my God.

(She sinks in a chair)

SONNY. You call those guys bums, Ma. But no one makes jokes about them. No one dares to, because they got money. They don't make you feel worse than... *dirt*... when you got money.

TONIA. You better wake up, figlio bello mio. You're a blind fool! You can't see it but I do, every night in my dreams. No! Not dreams, *nightmares*. You're gonna end up dead, Sonny. They're gonna kill you like some dog in the street and not even waste the time to spit on you.

SONNY. *(Shouts)* Stop! Will you just stop! Wait til I get the money. They're gonna give me respect. *That's* what I'll get.

TONIA. I don't understand. I don't know what to say anymore. Even your seventeen year old sister... she's got more brains. She's got more sense of responsibility.

SONNY. *(He wheels on her)* Oh, yeah? Where *is* Angie, Ma?

TONIA. With your grandmother. Why?

SONNY. Oh, she is, huh?

TONIA. She took her buy shoes.

SONNY. Oh, yeah? They sell shoes at DePasquale's?*

TONIA. It's a ristorante... DePasquale's.

SONNY. I know it's a restaurant. I was there this afternoon.

TONIA. Oh. You were there! You said there was an accident on the bridge. That's why you were late.

SONNY. I – uh... I had to see a guy.

* De - pas - qualls, no "e" on ending

TONIA. Ah. And what else did you see?

SONNY. I saw Angie. But I didn't see no Nonie.

TONIA. Did you talk to Angie? Did she say anything about Nonie?

SONNY. Angie didn't see me.

TONIA. Because you didn't want her to see you, you sonofa...

(Bites her knuckle. Crosses to statue and apologizes.)

Sant'Antonio mio... What I was gonna call my own son. Forgive me.

TONIA. *(con't) (She turns to Sonny)* Go! Go look and see if Nonie is in her bedroom. Maybe she's asleep.

(Sonny exits angrily. Dominic and Nicky enter. Nicky sits on the daybed with his book. Dominic, carrying fresh greens from the garden, wears a white handkerchief knotted at the corners for a hat. He crosses to the sink.)

DOMINIC. *(In greeting. Removes his "hat.")* Eh. Tonia.

TONIA. Dominic... come stai?

(Her mind is still on Sonny)

DOMINIC. Non ce malo*... non ce malo.

(He rinses greens. Sonny enters from bedroom)

SONNY. She ain't in there.

TONIA. Then go down to DePasquale's and find Angie. Bring her home.

SONNY. I got things I gotta do.

TONIA. I said... find Angie and bring her home. NOW!

(Sonny, shakes his head and curses to himself as he exits. Dominic, at sink, places greens in colander. He has been listening to the exchange)

TONIA. Nicky, you didn't see your grandmother after she went with Angie this afternoon?

NICKY. No, Ma. Isn't she at Gooma Regina's?

TONIA. Not when it's time for mangia.

---

* *NON chee ma - lo (not bad)*

(To Dominic)

You see your mother this afternoon when you got home from work?

DOMINIC. No. Nicky say she went to get the shoes with Angie.

TONIA. Nicky, go down Front Street right now. All the way to State Street. See if you can find Nonie. Look inside the stores. Especially the bakeries. You know how she hangs around until they give her a free cannoli.

(Nicky rises. Begins to leave)

Aspetto! Put the shoes. There's broken glass on the corner.

NICKY. It's too hot for shoes.

TONIA. PUT THE SHOES!!

NICKY. *(Picks up his sandals and carries them out, grumbling loudly)* You're not supposed to wear shoes in the summer.

DOMINIC. DePasquale's? Whatta she do there?

TONIA. *(Crosses to phone)* Wait a minute, Dominic. Maybe she is at the Comare's house. She goes almost every day for coffee.

DOMINIC. *(Does not like Comare Regina, so he reacts with a loud)* Eh-h-h-h!

TONIA. *(At phone, she dials five digits and listens)* Hello? Comare? Come stai? It's Tonia. Buona... buona. Comare, have you seen Nonie this afternoon?

(She listens)

Oh. It's time to mangiare*, and my mother-in-law is always here when's time to mangiare. Will you call me if you see her? Grazie.

(She listens)

Si, we'll be at the at the novena tonight. Ciao, Comare.

(She hangs up)

*mon - JAH - re (to eat

DOMINIC. Now the whole Front-a-Street-a is gonna know. That Gooma Regina gotta moutha bigga like-a jack-ass! You tell her one thing-a, and she tell tutti la monde.*

(Dominic removes a gallon jug of red wine from the space beside the refrigerator. He takes a cheese glass down from the shelf, sits at center of table.)

TONIA. *(Eyes him with disapproval)* Did Dr. Pareti say you can have that now?

DOMINIC. *(Pouring the wine)* He say one glass is ho-kay.

TONIA. M-m. He said one glass, once in a while. Not every day. You had some yesterday, too.

DOMINIC. Leave me 'lone.

TONIA. Dr. Pareti says with your condition…

DOMINIC. Dr. Pareti! He don't know nothing-a. I see him at the Bond Hotel last month and he drink like a fish.

TONIA. Dr. Pareti can drink like a whale if he wants. He doesn't have the enlarged heart!

DOMINIC. Tonia, please. I can't eat dis; I can't eat dat. He say no salt; I don't eat salt. He say no pork; I don't eat pork. Manga'na* piece da cake!

(Raises glass defiantly)

But I gotta have 'na bicchiere* di vino. It's good for the heart and makes the blood strong. If I cannot have the wine anymore, you might as well call D'Esopo Funeral Home, tell them to put me in the box and take me straight to the cemetery! We all gotta go there sooner or later anyway! So… per piacere". Let me enjoy a little!

(Raises his glass to her, and drinks)

TONIA. Eh! Drink!

(She crosses to door and looks out on porch)

Where the hell are they?

DOMINIC. Stop worry for my mother, will you? We live so many years on Front Street, she's not gonna get lost.

---

* *MAHN - ga - na (not even)*
* *bee - KEER - ee (glass)*
* *pee - ah - CHAD - YA, Long "a" (please)*

TONIA. *(Crosses to table and sits)* Dominic, what are we gonna do? Your mother is getting worse all the time.

DOMINIC. Whatta you mean? We do the same thinga we do every day.

TONIA. Now it is summer. Nicky watches her all day. In the fall, he goes back to school. And we all gotta work. She has changed so much in the last six months. Listen to this. How many years I been putting the mangia* in front of her? The other day, when I give her the plate she says, "What a nice lady. Who are you?"

(She leans forward)

Who *are* you? Dominic! We are not going to be able to leave her alone anymore.

DOMINIC. She getta a little confuse. She be all right.

(Sips his wine)

TONIA. *(Rises in anger)* She's *not* gonna be all right. She is getting too old.

DOMINIC. You worry for nothing-a. In the old country, my grandmother lived to be ninety-five or ninety-six.

TONIA. Oh. And did your grandmother go around scaring the hell out of everyone doing like this?

(She makes the sign-of-the-horns in his face. He pushes her hand away)

Her mind is going. When are you going to face this thing?

DOMINIC. She be ho-kay.

TONIA. What about this? She **peed** the chair over there.

(Crosses and picks up cushion. Holds it close to his face.)

Feel! Poor Nicky tried to clean it up so we don't know.

DOMINIC. Fa niente. *(Pushes pillow away forcefully)*

TONIA. *(Tosses pillow back on chair)* Last week she peed the bed. Before that on the porch. That's nothing, too?

DOMINIC. Eh. She make an accidente... that's all. She wait

---

* mahn - JAH *(food)*

too long to go.

TONIA. Jeus, Guiseppe e Maria!

(She exhales loudly in exasperation. A beat)

You got paid today. Where's your pay?

DOMINIC. On the shelf.

(Tonia crosses to shelf and picks up brown pay envelope. She extracts the few bills and some coins. Counts to herself. She looks at him)

TONIA. Where's the rest?

DOMINIC. That's all. Tutti.

TONIA. Tutti, shit. You take money out again. Every week you take the money. You steal from your own family.

(Holds out the meager remainder)

How am I gonna pay the rent with this? The bills for your doctor, the house, we support your mother completely... .and the mangia cost!

DOMINIC. Eh. Whatta you want from me? I bring you the envelope, no?

TONIA. You bring home the envelope, yes, but not one week you bring home all the money. You take the food right out of our mouths. What did you do with the money?

DOMINIC. Niente. I did nothing.

TONIA. You sent it to Italy.

DOMINIC. How am I gonna send?

TONIA. You think I'm a fool? You send it to your sister in the paese.

DOMINIC. It's war time. They don't bring the mail.

TONIA. They bring the mail. Mike Scorso, he got a letter from Italy.

(Drives it home)

He said to tell you that... your... sister... got... the money.

DOMINIC. It wasn't so much.

TONIA. Then what did you do with the rest!

DOMINIC. Leave me 'lone!

TONIA. You spent it on *yourself.* And your sister.

DOMINIC. All-a time my sister... my sister! She needs help, too. They got nothing over there. They go barefoot! **Managgia*** Mussolini!

TONIA. They went barefoot before Mussolini, so nothing is different. And you can say damn Mussolini all you want but it doesn't put the money back in our pockets.

I try so hard to save. We got to get out of this place some day. The street is getting more and crowded. More rundown.

(She steels herself)

Last week... I went to look at some nice places in East Hartford.

DOMINIC. *(Shouts) Go.* Look all you want. Because you go by yourself. When I leave-a diss house, it's gonna be feet first.

TONIA. We gotta get out of here. It's not like it used to be in the old days. And then, there's the bums.

DOMINIC. Bums? Where's the bums? You're crazy!

TONIA. You think Sonny is running around with the St. Joseph church choir? And I don't suppose two houses over... upstairs over Balesano's Fish Market... there's no puttana that lives there?

DOMINIC. *(Quietly)* Who?

TONIA. Maria La Brutta.

DOMINIC. The only thing-a wrong with Maria La Brutta is that she got six fingers on one hand. They call her "la brutta"... uga-ly... because of that. But she is not uga-ly.

TONIA. I am not talking about her finger. I am talking about that she is a puttana.

DOMINIC. How do you know? You see?

TONIA. She charges five dollars to do the "job" for the

---

* *mahn - AH - gee - ah (damn it)*

man.

DOMINIC. Five dollars.

(Begins to take a sip of wine)

That's not too bad.

TONIA. Bestia animale! That's all you men think of.

DOMINIC. Tonia, the man who goes to Maria LaBrutta, needs Maria LaBrutta. She is not the first whore in the world. They even got 'em in the Bible. So leave her alone. She keep-a to herself. She don't bother you.

TONIA. She bothers me. I see the men who go there. Everything around here bothers me. We gotta get away.

DOMINIC. For what? This is our home.

TONIA. I cannot do it alone while you steal from your family. Dominic, we gotta do it for Nicky. I'm afraid it's too late for Sonny. Even if we moved a thousand miles away, he would still find those bums. The gambling is a sickness with him. He can't leave it alone. But we gotta try. I'm afraid… he's gonna end up dead.

DOMINIC. Eh! Where da hell you get deez crazy ideas? Besides, it's his life. He didn't want to listen to me from when he was a kid.

TONIA. But Angie… she's gonna get married pretty soon and make a life of her own.

DOMINIC. Whatta you talkin' about? She don't even gotta no boyfriend.

TONIA. She's got a boyfriend.

DOMINIC. NO!

(Pounds the table)

She don't have no boyfriend unless I say. I pick him out when the time comes. We will make the match.

TONIA. This is not the old country. Angie will pick her own.

DOMINIC. Silenzio!

(His breath catches and he chokes)

I say… I will make the match.

TONIA. Don't get excited, please. We will see. You and me, we're gonna talk about this tonight, but you calm down first. Capeesh?

DOMINIC. NO! YOU capeesh… notta me!

(He crosses slowly to refrigerator and returns the bottle)

TONIA. Dominic, we are going to have to leave Front Street sooner or later. You mark my words. I feel it coming… in my bones.

DOMINIC. Eh-h-h! You and your magic-a bones! This street was here from when the first people came off the boats from the old country. They make another little Italia, right here on the river. Here we can walk up and down the street, day or night, just like in Napoli. We gotta alla the stores Italiana… alla the little push-a carts on both sides of the street. Here we can buy castagna, lemon-ice, gelati, toroni, tortoni, zeppola, baccala… tutti cosi! This place is just like Naples. You don't even gotta speak Enga-leesh if you don't wanna. They will **never** take this place away. You just tell your bones they are crazy.

TONIA. We'll see. And… my Nicky is gonna go to the *college.*

DOMINIC. Eh-h. Colleg-ia is for the rich people. Not for us. You gotta have the moneta.

TONIA. I will get it.

DOMINIC. What are you gonna do? Robba da bank? Tonia, let him get his hands dirty for once. It's not gonna hurt him. You keep him like a ba-by.

TONIA. Are you blind? Can't you see he is not like the others? He is special. *Special!*

DOMINIC. Strange. *Strange!* Thatsa what he is. You make him to be different. It'sa no good. Chase him outside for once.

TONIA. To get in trouble with those kids that got nothing to do? Look out on the street and see those boys playing crap right out in front of the polizia*.

---

* *pol - i - ZEE - ah*

DOMINIC. Then if you don't want him to go outside, make him go to work. Always he stays alone and writes in the book. The only friend he's got is that stoonato… John Malucci!

(Raises pointed fingers at her)

What does he write this-a book?

TONIA. You want to see what he writes?

(She crosses to notebook, opens to a page and hands it to him)

DOMINIC. *(Takes the book hesitantly. Looks at page. Squints at it. Obviously has great difficulty reading; long pauses between each word.)*

My-ya… dog-ga… Sheep.

TONIA. Shep.

DOMINIC. *(Puzzled)* But he don't gotta no dogga!

TONIA. He is writing about a dog. You don't have to have one to know about it.

DOMINIC. Tsk. Tsk. Tsk.

(Squints at page again)

These lines is funny. Some are short, some are long, some are long, some are short!

TONIA. That's a pome. But it's not finished yet.

DOMINIC. A *POMBA*!

TONIA. Stupido. A pomba! That's an **ENEMA**!

(She turns away in disgust)

I said a **pome**… which is great writing!

DOMINIC. Eh!

(Slaps the book shut and pushes it at her)

Can you eat this *pome?*

TONIA. Eat. That's all you think about. If you can't eat it, it's no good.

DOMINIC. A *pome* keeps your belly from growling?

TONIA. No. But you can stand it better if you got the pome

---

* POM-BA, with long "o"

inside you.

(She touches her breast)

Here.

DOMINIC. Tu si motta. Crazy. You complain about the money, but you talk about the pome, and you want me to plant the rose and the zinnia instead of the food we need for the table.

TONIA. Just a few plants. What's it gonna kill? You know I like to have few flowers for the house.

DOMINIC. Where you had the zinnia, I put in six pepper plants. *(Sips his wine)*

TONIA. You took out my zinnia? You took out my plants? Managgia diavolo!

(Rushes to door and looks out at the garden)

DOMINIC. The flowers bring the beetle Giaponese*. They eat the grape vines.

TONIA. Oh. The grape vines don't bring the beetles by themselves? Maybe we should cut them down because the beetles eat my flowers.

DOMINIC. What are you talkin' about? We gotta have the grapes for the wine.

TONIA. Because the wine goes into the stomach. Si?

DOMINIC. Si!

(Holds glass up to her, and takes another sip)

TONIA. I can't stand anymore.

(Crosses to door)

I'm gonna go look outside. Maybe I'll see somebody.

(She exits. Dominic turns in his chair to make sure she's out of the room. He rises, crosses to the radio and turns it on)

RADIO ANNOUNCER. City parks were jammed yesterday for the July 4th holiday as thousands…

(Dominic changes the station. We hear static and then

---

* Jap - o - NAYZ

circus music)

CIRCUS BARKER. Children of a-l-l ages! The Ringling-Brothers, Barnum & Bailey Circus brings to you the greatest performance in the history of the Greatest Show on Earth!

(Dominic has crossed to door and peeks out to make sure he is still alone)

Two days only! Wednesday, July 5th and Thursday, July 6th, with afternoon and evening performances.

(Dominic is back at the radio. Moves the dial.)

RADIO ANNOUNCER. Army Air Corps B-17 bombers hit strategic targets in Germany General Curtis LeMay announced today in...

DOMINIC. Managgia Mussolini!

(He changes the dial until he finds some lively Italian music. Satisfied, his head bobs up and down in time with the music. Now he crosses to open cupboard and reaches behind a stack of plates. He pulls out a small white confection bag. He opens it, removes a candy and pops it into his mouth, counting the remaining pieces silently. Folds up the bag and shoves it in his pocket. He takes cookie jar down and removes a biscotti and sticks it in his mouth; still keeping time with music. His back is to the door, but he hears Tonia enter. He tosses the biscotti back into the jar, clamps the lid on and tries to swallow what is in his mouth. Tonia has seen.)

DOMINIC. Did you see Mamma?

TONIA. Just Pietro selling vegetables from the wagon. Go ahead and eat. I don't want any mangia. I'm gonna go down to the river and look. The way she's been lately, she probably fell in.

DOMINIC. You stay here. I go look.

TONIA. You shouldn't walk too much in this heat

DOMINIC. I go easy... easy.

TONIA. Dominic. Please!

DOMINIC. It's cooler outside than it is in here!

TONIA. Dr. Pareti says you should not do too much in the heat. You already went to work today, and worked in the yard. That's enough.

DOMINIC. Tonia! Please. For one time, let me be a man.

TONIA. You are a man.

DOMINIC. No! I have not been a man for ten years. And when I could still be a man, you would not let me.

TONIA. Oh, my God. After all these years, you're gonna talk about that.

DOMINIC. You never want to talk about it, but I never stop thinking about it.

TONIA. We're too old for this stuff. Stop.

DOMINIC. When is the last-a time you even let me kiss you?

TONIA. I kiss the kids. That's enough.

DOMINIC. *(Beckons to her)* Veni qui.

TONIA. For what?

DOMINIC. I'm gonna kiss you.

TONIA. Oh, my God! Someone's gonna see!

DOMINIC. They gonna see a man kiss his wife… that's all.

TONIA. It's only the middle of the afternoon.

DOMINIC. The *sun*… or the *moon*… was *never* in the right place for you. Why?

(A beat)

Why??

TONIA. Because you never asked. You took!

(Quietly controlled)

You're right, Dominic. It is too hot in here. Go look for your mother.

DOMINIC. *(His mission is justified)* Don't worry. I'm going. I'm going.

(Looking back at her accusingly, he exits. Tonia turns her back to him, crosses to the radio and turns up the volume to drown out the sounds in her mind. She stands

there listening, but not hearing. Tonia is still standing by the counter with her back to the door, the radio blaring. Rocco appears in the doorway from the front hall, and knocks. She does not hear him over the radio. He knocks louder.)

ROCCO. Tonia!

(She does not hear)

TONIA!

(He steps into the room and shouts over the music)

TONIA. *(Startled, she jumps)* Jesu-Mari!

ROCCO. Can I come in?

(He crosses to table He wears his hat, and carries his jacket slung over one shoulder)

TONIA. *(Turns off radio)* My God... you scared me!

(Rocco removes his hat, and hangs his jacket on chair)

ROCCO. I'm sorry. I didn't mean to frighten you. I... I just stopped by from work. To tell you... hello.

TONIA. *(Indifferently)* Hello.

ROCCO. You look tired.

TONIA. Eh.

ROCCO. Can I sit down?

TONIA. *(Shrugs)* Sit.

ROCCO. Grazie.

(Pulls out chair and sits at table)

Where's Compa* Dominic?

TONIA. He went to look for his mother. She went somewhere with Angie and didn't come home yet.

ROCCO. Oh. She'll come home.

TONIA. *(Crosses to refrigerator and removes jug of wine)* You think so? You know so much.

ROCCO. Tonia, why are you so cruel to me?

TONIA. *(Gets glass off shelf and sets it in front of him)* I told you

---

* *COOM - bah*

not to come here anymore.

ROCCO. How can I not come here anymore? We are neighbors, and besides, Dominic's father and my father were compari di San Giovanni. It would look funny.

(Tonia shrugs and pour him wine)

You never allow me to be alone with you.

(Tonia puts a biscotti on a plate)

Why don't you want me to come here anymore? I haven't done anything.

TONIA. I don't like the way you look at me.

ROCCO. How do I look at you? I look at you with my eyes.

TONIA. It's what's behind the eyes I don't like.

(She leans over him to serve the biscotti. Rocco closes his eyes and inhales deeply)

TONIA. Hey! What is that? What are you doing?

ROCCO. I like your scent.

TONIA. It's very unusual. It's called Green Tobacco and Sweat.

ROCCO. You smell good. Like a woman.

TONIA. You should know.

ROCCO. What is that supposed to mean?

TONIA. Niente.

(She sits. A beat. Coyly.)

Do I smell like Maria LaBrutta?

ROCCO. No. She smells too strong of lily-of-the-valley. The last time I was there... ...

(Catches himself. A couple of beats.)

Oh, oh.

TONIA. Si. Oh, oh.

ROCCO. You know?

TONIA. I see you go there. Why don't you get married?

ROCCO. Why should I get married?

TONIA. At least you could go to a decent woman. Not a

puttana.

ROCCO. If I go to a decent woman, she will think that I am going to marry her in the end. I don't want to marry anyone. Besides, if I went to a decent woman, you would call her puttana, too.

(He paces)

And that Maria La Brutta? She's not so bad. Not like you think.

TONIA. You are a pig.

ROCCO. NO! I am a man. And a man has his needs. You won't admit it, but you have these needs, too.

TONIA. Not me.

(She jumps to her feet)

ROCCO. Tonia, the love between a man and woman is beautiful.

TONIA. Beautiful, shit.

(Makes a dusting-off motion with her hands)

It's bing-bang… good-bye, Jack… pull up the pants and go.

ROCCO. Scuzi, signora. What I meant to say is that the love between a man and a woman *should* be beautiful.

TONIA. If it's so beautiful, get yourself a wife. I don't want to talk about this anymore. Shut up.

(Places biscotti in front of him)

Eat.

ROCCO. I am not hungry… for food.

TONIA. Sporcaccione*! You'd better go!

ROCCO. I am sorry! I am sorry! I don't know what it is. Every time I see you, you do this to me. Like you want to punish me. I did not come here to do this.

TONIA. Why did you come here?

ROCCO. To tell you something.

TONIA. No more dirty talk?

ROCCO. Signora. I *never* talk dirty. And never to you! I

* Spork - ah - CHONE

swear on the holy saints. I respect you like... like... the Blessed Virgin. I would kiss your feet!

TONIA. You kiss anything, I break your teeth.

ROCCO. Please. Tonia. For God's sake... I got to tell you this before Dominic comes back.

TONIA. So... tell me.

ROCCO. I talked to my cousin this morning. Dominic's boss.

TONIA. Si?

ROCCO. They are going to let Dominic go. At the end of the month.

TONIA. Oh, my God.

ROCCO. They don't want to but he can't do the work anymore. His heart. When he tries to wash the bus or clean the inside, he gets the pains. And he has to sit down. He has had to sit down more and more each day, and the big bosses watch him.

TONIA. I know. Dominic should not even be working. Dr. Pareti says that his heart is so enlarged that one day soon... finito!

ROCCO. He can get Social Security. But there is no pension. He hasn't worked at the car barn long enough.

(Places his hand on Tonia's shoulder)

You are going to need help. I can help you.

TONIA. *(Shrugs him off)* Grazie. We will manage.

ROCCO. We are friends for so many years. You can accept my help. Don't be so foolish.

TONIA. And what do I have to do to pay you back for this help?

ROCCO. Niente! Now you really insult me!

(He walks away and then turns back)

I just ask that we can still be friends. That I can still come here and talk to you once in a while. Is that so much?

TONIA. See? I told you it costs.

(She sits)

ROCCO. *(Crosses to her and kneels on one knee)* Tonia, I'll never forget the day your father brought you here from Naples.

TONIA. What's wrong with you? Get up.

ROCCO. I thought you were the prettiest thing I ever saw. It was the eyes… dark, and so shy.

TONIA. My eyes! Pazzo. I said *get up*.

ROCCO. All right. I'm up.

(He rises.)

He brought you to the picnic for the Society of Maria della Grazie. There was food, music, dancing… boci… even a baseball game. But after you got there, I didn't see anything, or anyone else. You had a blue dress.

TONIA. Eh. I don't remember. Blue… green… What's the difference!

ROCCO. Blue.

TONIA. It was green! I don't remember.

ROCCO. I also remember that your marriage was already arranged with Dominic, even before you got to this country.

TONIA. *That,* I remember.

ROCCO. He was too old for you! Your father was crazy.

(Taps his head with his finger)

Why didn't you fight him?

TONIA. I was afraid of him. He would have killed me; or hit my mother again.

(She jumps up)

I had to be *very* careful. If he thought I did something wrong, he would hit me first, and then go after my mother. We had to do everything the men told us. Besides, making the match was the custom. We didn't know any better.

ROCCO. I have always wondered what it could have been if… Did you love Dominic right away?

TONIA. Love. The first time I was ever alone with him was on my wedding night. Whatever love I could have had was killed that same night.

ROCCO. Oh-h-h. Signora, I am very sorry.

(They look into each others eyes. There is a long pause)

TONIA. *(Quietly)* Rocco, I want you to leave this house now and don't come back anymore. Capeesh?

(Before Rocco can speak, the telephone rings)

(It rings three times before Tonia crosses to pick it up)

TONIA. Hello? Hello? Who is this?

(No response)

I hear you breathing you sonofabitch. Don't call here anymore or I'm going to call the police.

(She slams the receiver down)

Those goddam kids drive me crazy. They call, but they don't say anything.

(Telephone rings again)

TONIA. Encore!

(Tonia starts for the phone but Rocco stops her)

ROCCO. Let me get it.

(He picks it up. Answers forcefully)

Hello?

(He listens)

Oh... Sonny... it is you. Aspetto.

(Rocco hands the phone to Tonia. Their fingers touch)

(They both react, but she pushes him away)

TONIA. *(Into the phone)* Sonny? No, PaPa is not here. He went out to look, too. Did you see Angie? No? Well, did you find Nonie?

(She listens)

Oh, my God. She had a shock? How am I going to tell Dominic?

(She listens)

Dio mio! Where are you now? Aspetto.

ROCCO. What has happened?

TONIA. Can you drive me to St. Francis Hospital right away?

ROCCO. Of course.

TONIA. *(Into phone)* You wait there, Sonny. The Compare is going to take me.

(Tonia hangs up, and hurriedly Rocco helps her clear table.)

ROCCO. Is she very bad?

TONIA. *(Removes apron)* I don't know anything. Sonny said they took her in the ambulance and he followed in his car.

TONIA. *(con't)* *(She looks down at her dress, and then up at the door in surprise)*
Oh. Look. This dress is dirty. I can't go… this… way…

(Enter Maria LaBrutta with Dominic. Her purse is over one arm while she assists Dominic with the other. Tonia and Rocco watch speechlessly)

ROCCO. *(Shocked)* Maria!

MARIA. Well. Justa don't stand there, for Chris'sake. Pull out a chair.

(Rocco, shaken from his stupor, helps her)

MARIA. *(To Tonia, who is still staring)* Well? Does he need the medicine, or something?

TONIA. Oh! Sant'Antonia mi… si. He needs a pill.

(She crosses to shelf and removes a pill from one of the many medicine bottles. Dominic places pill under his tongue while they watch.)

TONIA. Dominic?

DOMINIC. *(He takes a few deep breaths and nods)* All right. I'm all right. Fa niente.

(He eyes her angrily)

TONIA. Do you want me to call Dr. Pareti?

DOMINIC. *Va ti favota, tu e Dr. Pareti.*

ROCCO. Compare! She is only trying to help you.

MARIA. You should not say things like that to your wife.

TONIA. Eh! I don't need *you* to defend me.

MARIA. Scuzi.

TONIA. Dominic, you go inside and lie down. You should stay quiet.

DOMINIC. How can I stay quiet when I see what you do?

TONIA. *(Bewildered)* What do I do?

DOMINIC. You know.

(Looks accusingly between Rocco & Tonia)

TONIA. No, I don't know. We don't have time to argue now. I was going to change my dress and go to the hospital.

DOMINIC. Why?

ROCCO. Because your mother... she fell down and they took her to St. Francis.

TONIA. Sonny is with her now.

DOMINIC. *(Eyeing them suspiciously)* Mamma? Da vera?

TONIA. Of course it's the truth!

ROCCO. I am going to drive her.

TONIA. Come on. You must lie down and rest.

DOMINIC. *(Pushing her hand away)* I go myself... easy... easy.

(Rises from chair and painfully makes his way to bedroom)

ROCCO. Let me help you, Compare.

DOMINIC. *(Shrugs him off)* **No!** Go! Go the hospital.

(He exits. There is an uncomfortable silence.)

TONIA. Rocco, I have to stay with him until he sleeps. Per piacere... I don't like to ask you but Sonny is waiting.

ROCCO. *(Glad to be leaving, retrieves his hat and jacket)* Don't worry about a thing. I will go and find Sonny, and when I find out what the story is, I will call you.

TONIA. Grazie.

ROCCO. Po ci vidiamo*.

(He exits hurriedly)

(There is an awkward silence. Tonia and Maria face each other and electricity bristles between them. Both women speak at the same time)

MARIA. Well, now that...

(She stops when Tonia speaks)

Excuse me.

TONIA. I suppose...

(She stops)

Scuzi.

(She concedes)

Go. You first.

MARIA. I just wanted to say, now that Dominic seems all right, I will go.

(She clutches her purse and starts for the door)

TONIA. Wait.

(Maria turns.)

(Throughout the following scene, Tonia never allows herself to get close to Maria. She keeps her distance; Maria knows her place).

MARIA. Si?

TONIA. *(With difficulty)* Thank you for helping him home.

MARIA. Fa niente.

(Turns to exit)

TONIA. Wait.

MARIA. Signora, please. Say what you want and get it over. I know you don't like to have me in your house.

TONIA. All right. I never expected this. You did us a favor. I am sorry. I was rude to you.

MARIA. And your husband was very rude to you, Signora.

---

* *Po chee vee - dee - AMO (see you later)*

TONIA. Eh. That is nothing new.

MARIA. *(With pity)* I know.

TONIA. You know?

> *(Her eyes wide, she circle Maria like an animal stalking its prey)*

What else do you know?

(Suddenly occurs to her)

Where did you find my husband?

MARIA. He was at my house… .when he felt ill.

TONIA. At *your* house!

MARIA. Oh, it's not what you think, Signora. Your husband is a sick man.

TONIA. I need you to tell me this?

MARIA. *(Matter-of-factly to ease the situation, but makes it worse.)* Oh, your husband has been coming to my house for years.

TONIA. What?

MARIA. But… not for what you think. A lot of men come to me… for… what you think. But not your husband.

TONIA. What *does* he come for?

MARIA. *(Matter-of-factly)* For my Zuppa Englese.

(She looks at her wrist watch)

TONIA. Scuzi. What did you say?

MARIA. For my Zuppa Englese.

(A beat.)

He likes my rum cake. Tu capeesh… *rum cake?*

TONIA. Jesu, Guiseppe e Maria. You expect me to believe that?

MARIA. *(Gestures with opens hands meaning "It's the truth.")* Eh!

TONIA. You mean to tell me that Dominic has been going to your house to eat *cake!*

MARIA. For years. Si.

(She gestures to chair)

Can I sit down, please. I got bad arches. They go down instead of up.

TONIA. *(No response. Maria sits anyway)* You mean, you just *give* my husband rum cake??

MARIA. Oh, no, signora. I sell it to him.

TONIA. For how much?

MARIA. I charge him the same as if he came for... the other.

TONIA. *(Furious)* Five dollars for a lousy piece of **cake?**

MARIA. Hey... I am not in the bakery business. When he comes and eats the cake, he takes up my valuable time. If I let him sit there and eat free cake, I lose money.

TONIA. I can buy five Zuppa Englese cakes for five dollars!

MARIA. Eh. Dominic wants to pay. I don't even have to ask. The first thing he does when he walks in, he puts his hand in his pocket.

(Tonia makes a sound of fury)

Signora, do you mind if I speak frankly?

TONIA. Nothing stopped you yet.

MARIA. Va bene. I know a lot of men over the years. Since the Depression... you know? Your husband is, let's say, very different... unusual.

TONIA. So what? Why should you care?

MARIA. I don't know. Maybe because your husband seems to get some kind of strange satisfaction from eating rum cake in the house of a putta... in my house. Every week now, for years, too many to count, two times a week sometimes, he comes. At least once a week. Thursday evening. Instead of going to the Holy Name meeting.

TONIA. That sonofabitch! No wonder he never told me anything about the meetings.

MARIA. He's got a lot of crazy, old fashioned ideas.

TONIA. And he tells you these ideas?

MARIA. He talks while he eats. With his mouth full, usually. I don't ask questions. I just listen. It's my job.

(Tonia laughs scornfully)

...to *listen*. No matter what some may think.

TONIA. And what do you hear, while you are performing this "listening" job?

MARIA. I hear... scuzi, you said I could speak freely.

TONIA. I said go ahead.

MARIA. I hear... that you don't have the... married life, shall we say?

TONIA. That is none of your goddam business!

MARIA. I am sorry. I am sorry.

TONIA. He is an animale... una bestia animale!

MARIA. Forget it, signora. Forget what I said.

TONIA. You better go. I already told you thank you.

(Threatening tone)

MARIA. All right. I am going.

(Takes her purse and rises)

But before I leave, I want to give you a little word of warning.

TONIA. When the hell did you become my guardian angel? I don't see no wings sticking out of your back.

MARIA. Eh!

(Throws up her hands and begins to exit)

It's up to you. This is about your son.

TONIA. *(Her eyes narrowed like slits)* What about my son? He likes your Zuppa Englese, too?

MARIA. No. No. It's about the men he runs around with. They are not boys, signora. They are men. No good. No good.

(She gestures with her gloved hand)

If you take my advice, make him stop running with them. They are big time. Not these little pipa-squeaks that run the numbers up and down Front Street. Those guys are small potatoes. Niente! But these other ones... no good.

TONIA. Do you know these men?

MARIA. Maybe. Maybe not. Not personally, if you know what I mean. But in my business... you'd be surprised how much I hear. Those men are not even from these parts. Capeesh?

TONIA. Eh, Sonny doesn't pay attention to me anymore.

MARIA. Make him listen! Rocco says you should take him by the neck and shake him until his teeth rattle.

TONIA. What has Rocco got to do with anything?

MARIA. Signora, one of the reasons I am trying to help you is because of Rocco. He thinks... molto bene... of you. For a long time I thought maybe there was a chance for us, but no! He never had eyes for me. I know him for years, you know.

TONIA. I know you know him for years. I see him go up and down your stairs over the Balesano Fish Market. A person would have to be blind to miss the path he has worn out on the paint.

MARIA. You are wrong about him. And you don't have to pretend with me. I know about Rocco.

TONIA. What about him?

MARIA. Your husband is very jealous. He has known for a long time.

TONIA. There is nothing to know. I have nothing to do with Rocco DelGrosso! He is a compare of my husband and he comes here once in a while to visit. That is all.

MARIA. You mean you have no feelings for Rocco?

TONIA. I told you, I have **nothing** for him. What do you think I am?

MARIA. Signora, life has a cruel habit of cheating us of our dreams. Who would blame you if you and Rocco...

(Wiggles her gloved hand in her face)

You know, I wouldn't want a husband like Dominic.

Don't misunderstand me. He's a nice man, but come on! He's a *gavone**.

TONIA. I am a good woman. I swear on the holy statue of Saint Anthony that I have been a pure wife. Not a **puttana.**

(She hisses in her face)

I have never… ever… put the horns on my husband, gavone or no!

MARIA. All I am saying is that Rocco is such a bell'uomo; so molto gentile. Who could blame a woman if she harbored any feelings for such a man?

TONIA. If Rocco told you this dirty thing, he's a *buschiardo**. A liar!

MARIA. No! No!

(Waving her gloved hand in her face)

Rocco never told me this. It was Dominic.

TONIA. And you believed that cornuto? That… ANIMALE!

MARIA. How am I supposed to know? He is the one who lives with you… no? Do you ever talk to me if you pass me on the street or see me at the market? No. You cross the street, or look the other way. I am a person, too! I've got feelings.

TONIA. GET… OUT… OF… MY… HOUSE… MARIA… LA… BRUTTA.

(In slow motion she reaches for the broom which is leaning against the wall near the refrigerator. She raises the broom in the air and stalks her)

And don't you never, ever wave that goddam hand in my face again or I will bite off your sixth finger and spit it in your puttana face!

(Clutching her purse, and trying to get to the door, she grabs the broom and the two women struggle at a stalemate. Maria would never use the broom against Tonia; instead she stops her with her words)

---

* *ga - VO - NE, with a long "o" (crude; without manners)*
* *boosch - i - AR - do (liar)*

MARIA. I came here to help you, and to bring your husband home, Signora DeLuna. But I think something is not right when the only thing that bothers you when your husband is with a puttana is that he spends money. But when I mention Rocco's, name you show the jealousy! Explain *that* one, Signora Tonia DeLuna!

(Maria gives Tonia one last shove and releases the broom, which enables her to get out of the door.)

(Tonia gets the door open and screams after her.)

TONIA. Now I know why you live over the fish market! Because you both stink alike! Brutta puttana! If you come back here again, I will break this broom over your back so hard you will have to do the job standing up for the rest of your life!

(She slams the door shut. Totally spent, she throws the broom to the floor, and trying to catch her breath, she collapses against the door frame.)

BLACK OUT!

End Act I

ACT II

Scene I

(It is the same evening, several hours later. As the lights come up, we hear the giggling and chatter of Angie and Victor as they ascend the porch. They are both a little tipsy. Victor holds the door open, removes his soldier's cap and performs a sweeping bow)

VICTOR. Apres vous, piccolina mam'selle.

ANGIE. That's not right, silly.

(She enters a bit unsteady on her feet)

You got a little mixed up there with your French and Italian.

VICTOR. I just love getting mixed up with a little Italian.

(He holds open his arms and she rushes into them.

He buries his nose in her hair and takes a long, slow breath.)

M-m-m. Angelina... Angelina... you smell quite suprema!

(A beat.)

Say! Do you realize that if you marry me your name will be *Angelina Frankelina*?

ANGIE. Oh, Victor. That's **awful**.

VICTOR. It's not **that** bad! How could you do this to a man who never thought of anyone else during those six long weeks of basic. Just ask me about those two juicy love letters I tore up and threw away from Rosemarie Spinelli! I mean... wow! Those letters were so hot, the ink steamed off the paper. H-m-m. Now, Rosemarie

Frankelina. That's got a pretty good ring to it, don't you think?

ANGIE. Well. I wasn't going to tell you this, but you're safe. Because my first name is Angela. Not Angelina!

(They rush into each other's arms. They hug and he whirls her around. Extricating herself, she looks around)

I wonder where everybody is?

(She calls.)

Mamma? I'm home. Mamma?

(She remembers.)

Oh... it's Wednesday. They're at the novena, and there's the Rosary after.

VICTOR. You mean... HA... HA... HA...

(He stalks her with arms raised, monster-style)

Ve... are... ALONE?

(She squeals as he clutches her. He picks her up and whirls her around again, carries her to a chair and sets her at the table)

ANGIE. Oh, my head. I never should have had that wine. I didn't like it. I don't even like the stuff my father makes.

VICTOR. When the waiter took you for twenty-one, you acted mighty pleased.

ANGIE. Tony? He knows I'm not twenty-one. He was treating us so nice because you're in the service and he heard you say you were shipping out on Saturday. That's when he came over with that carafe of red wine.

VICTOR. You had only one glass, but I did my duty like a red-blooded American G.I. and drank he rest of it. But you know something, Angie, I don't need any wine.

(Tenderly)

You're better than anything that comes in a bottle. The first time I was with you, it just felt *right*. Like we belonged together. You snuck into my mind and I kept seeing your face and hearing your voice wherever I went. You're the first thing I think of every morning and the last thing every night. Sounds crazy, but I can't get enough of having you near me, to see you or touch you. But it's wonderful crazy. This time next week, who knows where I'll be... I just don't want our time together to end yet.

(He leans toward her and they kiss gently on the lips. Then he removes a rolled up newspaper from his back pocket. Wistfully.)

So, what do you say? Let's take in a movie.

ANGIE. Oh, Victor. I feel the very same way.

(Caresses his face.)

But my mother won't let me go out tonight, too. It's enough that she let me spend the afternoon with you. You are the only boy that I have ever brought home. I was scared, but she said she'd prepare my father. You don't know what he can be like.

VICTOR. He's just going to have to get used to it, Angie. He's going to be seeing a lot of this face around here after the war. After all, you're my girl... aren't you Angie?

ANGIE. I'm your girl.

VICTOR. And we haven't done anything wrong, have we?

ANGIE. Of course not.

VICTOR. If I promise to bring you right home after the movie, your mother will let you go.

ANGIE. I suppose so.

VICTOR. You know what I would like to see? A good shootem-up Western! That'll take our minds off the war, at least for a couple of hours.

ANGIE. God, I hate this war. You haven't talked about it much... but... are you scared?

VICTOR. Sure, I'm scared. Not much about the fighting because they train us pretty doggone good for that.

And I try not to think about the dying part, because that doesn't do anyone any good. But I really am scared about all of the things I might be missing... things in our future. Things I pictured *us* sharing, Angie.

ANGIE. We will share them, Victor. I just know it. You're the only one I have wanted to share those things with, too.

(They hug. She pushes him gently to the couch and kneels at his feet.)

Do you know one of the biggest reasons I care for you so much?

(Victor shakes his head)

You didn't laugh at me when I said I wanted to save myself... you know... for my husband. You didn't say I was dumb or naive. You didn't say "everybody's doing it... especially with their boyfriends going overseas"... and all. Or... "That way, you *really* belong to me."

(He pulls her close and kisses her cheek)

I mean, I want to Victor. But I think we are so special. And if I had to tell it in confession... we wouldn't be special anymore. Just like all of the others.

VICTOR. God, Angie. How could I laugh when it's ME you're saving yourself for? It's going to be a long way off yet, but I know it's going to a wedding night to remember. And you know what else, Ang?

ANGIE. What?

VICTOR. I was afraid that you were going to laugh at me because I felt the very same way.

(He holds her close)

I love you, Angelina. God. How I love you.

(They kiss and back themselves onto the daybed until they are reclining. They continue to hug and kiss and murmur to each other.)

(Dominic enters. He is carrying an empty water glass as he heads for the sink. He passes them without seeing them,

puts the glass down, and turns. He stops dead when he sees them. They are not aware of him as they embrace.)

DOMINIC. WHATTA... THE..HELL... DO... YOU... TINK... YOU... ARE... DOIN'??

VICTOR. *(Leaping to his feet)* Oh, my gosh!

ANGIE. PaPa! I didn't know you were home!

(She scrambles to her feet)

DOMINIC. I can see dat.

(Moves in)

Who is diss?

ANGIE. This is Victor.

DOMINIC. Victor! Victor who?

ANGIE. Didn't Mamma tell you?

DOMINIC. Mamma? Does she know about diss?

ANGIE. Yes. She said she was going to tell you.

DOMINIC. You. Victor. Get out.

VICTOR. Wait, Mr. DeLuna. I know this looks bad but it's not what you think. I love Angie.

DOMINIC. I know what you love.

ANGIE. Pa... listen. Please! Victor and I didn't do anything.

DOMINIC. You been drinking. I can smell it from here. Tu s'umbriago*!

ANGIE. I'm not drunk. I had one glass of wine...

(Dominic draws nearer)

DOMINIC. You shut your moutha. Tu si 'na puttana... the same thing just like your Mamma.

ANGIE. PaPa! What are you saying?

(She is crying)

DOMINIC. Where did you pick him up? On the street?

(He slaps her across the face. She screams and reels backward.

Victor calls out to her and rushes to help her up)

* soom - bree - AH - go (drunk)

VICTOR. *(Furious)* Angie hasn't done anything. She's a good girl, Mr. DeLuna. You have no right to do this.

(Dominic is at the kitchen drawer. With great deliberation he opens the drawer and rummages. He pulls out a butcher knife, turns to **VICTOR.** *and threatens him with it.)*

DOMINIC. Get outta diss house… soldier… whatever your name is… from the street…

ANGIE. PaPa! My God. What are you doing?

(Crying hysterically)

(Sonny enters from the back porch but stops short when he sees what is happening.)

SONNY. PAPA!!

(Everyone freezes)

Give me the knife.

DOMINIC. NO! NO!

SONNY. *(Holds out his hand for the knife)* Hear me? GIVE ME THE KNIFE.

(Dominic never takes his eyes off of Victor but he gives up the knife)

What the hell is wrong with you! Have you lost your mind? Rocco said you were sick tonight. What are you trying to do? Your going to make yourself drop dead with all this excitement.

DOMINIC. You shoulda see what they was-a doing. They was doing the jobba… on the couch! They didn't think nobody was home. She's a puttana… just-a like… a…

(Angie cries hard)

SONNY. PA!

(He turns to Angie who continues crying throughout the scene)

For Chris-sake, Angie. Stop the crying, will ya? Nobody can hear.

(Crosses to her and attempts to comfort her)

Hey. We know you're okay, but I think your friend better go now.

VICTOR. But it's not fair. He's making it look terrible. We haven't done anything wrong.

SONNY. *I said... you'd better go.*

(Then, gently)

Go on.

(Victor takes his cap, looks at Angie, Dominic, Sonny and back to Angie. He exits)

SONNY. Come on, Pa. You'd better get back to bed. You know what the doctor said.

DOMINIC. She don't have no boyfriend unless I say.

SONNY. This ain't the old country, Pa!

(Steers him toward his room)

DOMINIC. Io sono il capo di questa casa! She don't have no boyfriend unless I say.

(Dominic moves towards the bedrooms.)

She don't have no boyfriend unless I say.

(He exits)

SONNY. *(Crosses to sink, wets towel.)* Here. Put this on your face.

(Angie applies it to her cheek. Sonny pulls out a chair.)

Here. Sit down.

ANGIE. *(Sobbing)* Oh, God, Sonny. I hate h-i-m. I'm so ***ashamed.***

SONNY. Sh-h. Come on, now. He's your father, huh? You know he ain't gonna change. Besides, what are you? Crazy... bringin' that guy here?

ANGIE. He isn't "that guy," Sonny. He's Victor. And we're practically engaged. Mamma knew about it. She knew! She was supposed to be here. This wouldn't have happened if she were here. Where was she? Huh? WHERE WAS SHE?

SONNY. Ma couldn't help it, Ang. Don't be mad at her. She's at the hospital with Nonie.

ANGIE. What? She's at the hospital?! Why?

SONNY. Nonie wandered off by herself this afternoon and fell. Why don't you try to pull yourself together and go sit with Ma at St. Francis.

ANGIE. Nonie was all right when I left her here. It's all my fault, isn't it, Sonny?

(She cries anew.)

SONNY. Now you're talking' crazy. It was nobody's fault. Nonie was gettin' more stoonato* by the day.

ANGIE. Is she going to be all right?

SONNY. It don't look too good. The doctors said she had a shock.

(Angie starts to cry all over again. Nicky runs up on the porch.)

Now... quiet, come on. Nicky's comin'.

(Nicky enters crying audibly and throws himself headlong on the couch.)

SONNY. Go in and get cleaned up, Angie. I'll drive you over, and then... I... uh... gotta see a guy. Okay? There's somethin' really big goin' on tonight.

(Angie exits)

SONNY. Now, what are *you* cryin' about?

(Seats himself beside Nicky.)

NICKY. *(Crying)* I was at John Malucci's and his mother just said that Nonie went to the hospital in the ambulance and that she had a shock. Father Guidone announced it at the novena.

SONNY. Come here. Sit up.

(Nicky sits up as Sonny gets him a glass of water.)

NICKY. It must have hurt her an awful lot. Bad enough to make her go to the hospital.

---

* stoon - AH - toe (addle-brained)

SONNY. Aw, no. There's no pain, chooch. The kind of shock that Nonie had is kinda nice. You don't feel nothin'. You just sorta get numb. Right now, she's sleepin' so peacefully.

NICKY. *(Choking back the tears)* Is Nonie going to die, Sonny?

SONNY. She's awfully old, Nick. You know... ..we can't keep people *forever*, don't you?

(Nicky nods)

No matter how hard we try. It's like... they're just *loaned* to us for a while.

NICKY. Oh, gee. But I love her, Sonny.

SONNY. I know. We all love that little old lady in the black dress and black stockings with that dumb rag around her grey hair. And out of all of us, *you've* always been her special favorite. You never could do anything wrong in her eyes!

NICKY. I don't care. I wish they could loan her to us a little longer.

SONNY. She was gettin' too old, Nick. You saw how she was peein' on everything. Ain't it better that she sleeps herself away than to have her come home and fall down again, and really hurt herself? And with the way things were goin', she'd pee a lot more on things. Just last week, when I came home from work, I saw this puddle on the back porch. And I said to Nonie, I said, "Nonie, did you do that?" I mean, I wasn't mad at her or anything. I said it real nice. "Nonie, did you do that?"

(He turns to Nicky)

And do you know what she answered?

NICKY. What?

SONNY. She said: "I didn't do it. The cat did it."

NICKY. But we don't have a cat.

SONNY. See? You know what I mean? You know how I want to remember Nonie?

NICKY. How?

SONNY. I want to remember her in this kitchen, singing those love songs in that squeaky voice of hers, and cooking for us like she loved to.

NICKY. That's how I'd like to remember her, too. I don't want to remember her only peeing on things. But I will always love her. I think I love her more now that she's had the shock.

SONNY. Me, too, chooch.

(Pull him close and kisses the top of his head)

Hey. Pa doesn't know about Nonie, yet. Let me be the one to tell him later, okay?

(Makes exaggerated gesture in the air and covers his pockets with his hands)

And now... Ladies and Gentlemen...

(Creates drum roll.)

NICKY. Aw, not again!

SONNY. Oh. You're getting too old for that, huh?

NICKY. I think so.

SONNY. I guess you're right.

(He takes two pieces of red cardboard from his pocket and hands them to Nicky)

NICKY. *(Reading quietly)* Sonny! Two tickets to the circus. Wow. *(Hesitantly)* But, I don't know if I want to go... now.

SONNY. Nonie would want you to go, Nick. She'd be the last person to expect you to sit around here, mopin'. You know how she was always runnin' up and down Front Street, lookin' for excitement. She'd be mad if you didn't go.

NICKY. You think so?

SONNY. I know so.

NICKY. Would be it all right if I asked John *Malucci* to go to the circus with me?

SONNY. Yeah. Sure. Go ask his mother. I'll straighten it out with Ma and Pa. But be back in one hour and stay with Pa tonight. And don't lose the tickets. They're for the matinee tomorrow afternoon.

NICKY. *(At door, he turns and reads from the tickets)* "Ringling-Brothers, Barnum & Bailey Circus. Thursday, July 6, 1944. For a day in your life you will never forget."

(He looks up)

Sonny? Thanks.

SONNY. Ah.

(Waves him off)

NICKY. Sonny?

SONNY. Now what?

NICKY. You know how Ma always says she wants me to be a lawyer, and Pa says I should be a farmer? And Nonie says a "big, rich doctor," and you think I should be a writer?

SONNY. What? You don't want to be one?

NICKY. Oh, I do. But is it okay if I want to be like you, too? If I say that to Ma, she yells her head off and says long swear words.

SONNY. Well, whatta you know. For once I agree with Ma. You chooch. If you ever get to be like me, I'm gonna punch you right in the panzone. Capeesh? Go on. Go with Malucci. Malooch and Chooch!

(Nicky exits. Alone, Sonny is about to cross to the couch to retrieve the stash of money. He is startled when Dominic enters from the hallway.)

Pa! What's the matter? You should be lying down.

DOMINIC. Eh, Mamma? How is... she?

SONNY. Oh, Pa.

(He crosses to Dominic and embraces him.)

DOMINIC. Morte. Si?

SONNY. Not yet.

(Dominic begins to weep silently)

DOMINIC. Mamma… oh, Mamma.
SONNY. Come on. Let's get you back to bed.
DOMINIC. I go myself… easy… easy.

(Weeping still, he turns and exits.)

(Alone now, Sonny returns to the couch, extricates the wad of money from the envelope from under the mattress, and shoves it in his pocket. He crosses to the coat rack, puts his hat on with a debonnaire twist, picks up his jacket and exits.)

End Act II (Scene I)

Scene II

(The next day, later afternoon. Angela enters. She is carrying a prayer book and on her head she wears a lace head scarf. There is a mark on her cheek, which she has tried to cover up with make-up. She removes the lace and sets it on the counter with the prayer book. The sound of the telephone ringing sparks the first sign of animation in her. She hurries to the phone.)

ANGELA. Hello?

(She is puzzled)

What? Is this you, Victor? Who has twenty minutes? Who is this?

(The other party hangs up)

Hello?

(Confused, Angie hangs up)

(Dominic enters from the bedroom. He is dressed in trousers and only his sleeveless underwear top.)

(Angela and Dominic look at each other but she turns away and begins to prepare her mother's coffee. She sets the pot on the burner)

DOMINIC. Did you go see your grandmother this morning?

(Angie does not answer. She takes a cup off of the shelf and puts it at Tonia's place)

DOMINIC. Hey! I'm-a talking to you.
ANGELA. *(Coldly)* I went.
DOMINIC. Are you gonna tell-a me how she is or not?
ANGIE. The same.
DOMINIC. I'm gonna put on a shirt.

(He exits and she glares in anger at his back. She wheels around and returns to stove to check the pot. She touches her cheek and winces from the tenderness)

(The Suitor comes up on porch and we see him behind the screen door. He is in his mid-thirties; very short, dark

with his hair slicked back. There is no part in his hair. His suit is ill-fitting; too short in the sleeves and trousers, and his socks are white. His shoes are run down and do not match the suit. His necktie is a young boy's and is much too short. It hangs off-center. He stands at the door looking at a little scrap of paper. He knocks at the door)

THE SUITOR. Scuzi?

ANGIE. *(Startled)* Oh…

(Crosses to door)

Hello. Are you lost? Who are you looking for?

THE SUITOR. *(Looks at paper and then back to her)* Is diss da casa di Dominic DeLuna?

ANGIE. Yes, this is where he lives.

SUITOR. I am un'amico di Dominic.

ANGIE. Oh. You're a friend of my fathers?

SUITOR. Si. A verra special-a one.

ANGIE. Well, please… come in.

(She opens the door. He enters and he ogles her lewdly.)

Do you speak English?

THE SUITOR. Yeah. I talk Enga-leesh pooty-gooda. No every-ting'a, tho. Ma… capeesh tutti cosi. Tu capeesh Italiano?

ANGIE. Si… yes. I understand. Uh… my father is changing his clothes. He'll be out in a few minutes.

(The Suitor grins at her and makes her very uncomfortable.)

ANGIE. It's… hot. Fa caldo.

THE SUITOR. Hey… hey… Whew! Whew!

(Pulls open his shirt and fans his neck)

THE SUITOR. Scuzi, signorina. Come si chiamo*? What is your name-a?

ANGIE. Angela. My name is Angela.

THE SUITOR. *(His eyes sparkle and he grins widely with the knowledge)* **YOU…** .are *Angela*? Ah! *Nice-sa… nice-sa.*

* Coo - ma see key - ah - mo

(Dominic enters. Sees his friend; they greet enthusiastically and embrace.)

DOMINIC. Eh… amico Come stai*?

THE SUITOR. Buona. Buona. E tu?

DOMINIC. Non chi malo*.

(Dominic pulls out a chair and motions to him)

Asetta*. Asetta.

(The Suitor sits and Dominic seats himself opposite)

DOMINIC. Angela, get the anisette.

(Angela glares angrily at him. She does not move at first. During the next scene, Dominic and The Suitor discuss friends they know from the old country.)

DOMINIC. Eh! How is that Salvatore Bucciccello… in Napoli?

THE SUITOR. Che e*… Salvatore Bucciccello?

DOMINIC. You know… the guy… who work on the rail-a-road.

THE SUITOR. Oh… esso morte!

DOMINIC. Morte? *(Shocked)* Mussolini?

THE SUITOR. Si! Mussolini!

DOMINIC & THE SUITOR. *(Both bite their fists and shout)* Managgia* Mussolini!

(Angela stomps over to the shelf and returns quickly with a bottle of anisette. She sets it down firmly in front of Dominic and returns to the stove)

DOMINIC. *(Turns to Angela)* Hey! Angela! We need the glasses. Whatta you thinka?

(Angela returns to the shelf.)

DOMINIC. *(To The Suitor)* Eh… what about that Giuseppe Falconetti?

---

* *Coo - ma STY (how are you friend?)*
* *NON chee ma - lo*
* *Ah - SET*
* *KEY - a, with long "a"*
* *Mahn - AH - gee - ia*

THE SUITOR. That chiacchierone* ... always with the mouth-a open... he talka... talka... talka? Esso morte, too!

DOMINIC. Morte? I didn't even know he wassa sick!

THE SUITOR. No! No sicka! MUSSOLINI!

DOMINIC & THE SUITOR. *(Both bite their fists and shout anew)* Managgia Mussolini!

(Angela now has taken down two very tall, extra large water tumblers and plants them down hard in front of Dominic. Dominic starts to speak to The Suitor but when he sees the glasses, he turns to Angela who is back at the stove)

DOMINIC. ANGELA!

ANGIE. WHAT!

DOMINIC. What the hella do you think you are doin'?

THE SUITOR. *(Holds up his hands to decline the drink and he makes a face to indicate that he does not like it)* Grazie. I no wanna anisette. I no like-a. Itsa too sweeta.

DOMINIC. Un poco! Un poco.

(Insisting, he pours.)

THE SUITOR. All right. Un poco. Allora.

(The drink, clinking glasses and saying "Salute!)

Eh, Dominic. I almost forgot! Dissa is da money for **la biancheria.***

(Pulls a large wad of bills out of his pocket)

DOMINIC. *(Dominic's lights up at the sight of the money)* Bravo!

ANGIE. That looks like a lot of money. You shouldn't flash it around. What's it for?

THE SUITOR. *(With a meaningful smile. Winks at her)* La... bianchieria.

ANGIE. A dowry?

---

* kyah - kyha - RO - NE, with long "o" (gossip; windbag)
* bee - yon - ka - REE - a (dowry)

THE SUITOR. *(With a satisfied smile)* Eh! You can call-a anyting-a you like.

ANGIE. Your bride-to-be is very lucky. *She's* supposed to supply the dowry, and here you are paying for it yourself.

THE SUITOR. *(In ecstacy)* Ah… nice-sa, nice-sa.

ANGIE. Who are you again? I don't think I heard your name.

THE SUITOR. Me? Io sono il aspirante.

ANGIE. Aspirante? Oh, Mr. Aspirante.

(Suddenly understanding)

ASPIRANTE? PA! You brought him here for me. How *could* you?

DOMINIC. You shut up. I tolda your mother that when the time came we would fa la maschiata* and the time came last night. *(Points at the couch)*

THE SUITOR. Si. Si. Makea la match-a. Nice-sa, nice-sa.

ANGIE. *(Begins to cry)* PA! Even if I did want him, he's too old for me.

DOMINIC. You be lucky to have this-sa guy. His wife just die and left him lots of property in Poquonock*. He was even-a all ready to go back to the old county for a bride.

(Angie cries louder)

I tell you, you be lucky to get him. He's got such a nice farm with l'animale… e tutti cosi!

THE SUITOR. Si. Witta an-i-mala. Due vacci*, due cavalli*…

(Holds up the appropriate number of fingers and on "three" he wiggles them)

E **tre** porci*.

(Makes loud oinking sounds. Angie cries harder)

ANGIE. PA! Why are you doing this to me? I thought you loved me!

---

* *masch - ee - AH - ta (to make a match)*
* *Poe - quon'ick (rural town outside of Hartford)*
* *VOCK - ee, cav - AH - lee (cows, horses)*
* *PORK - ee (pigs)*

(Tonia enters. Sets purse on the counter)

TONIA. My God, there's a big fire someplace in the north end. We can see the smoke from the tobacco bus. The sirens go crazy. Did you... ?

(She sees Angie's tears, and the visitor)

Hello? What is this?

ANGIE. MA! PaPa brought this man here to fa la maschiata. For ME! I'll kill myself first. I'll run away and kill myself.

TONIA. *(Tenderly. Pushes her into the rocking chair.)* You... shut up.

(To Dominic, she speaks pleasantly, smiling and nodding to the suitor all the while)

Dominic, this is true?

DOMINIC. Maybe he's got a few years on him. No more than you and me and look how fine we do.

TONIA. *(Sardonically)* Oh... sure!

DOMINIC. She don't wanna listen how lucky she be to get this guy. Maybe he don't speaka Inglesa so good but he gotta nicesa bigga farm, and look at the moneta he bring for her biancheria.

TONIA. *(Crosses to back of Dominic's chair and places her hand on it. She leans towards his ear, still smiling pleasantly)*

You tell your friend...

(Smiles at The Suitor)

...that... you... made... a... mistake, eh?

(To The Suitor)

Scuzi. Mia marito make a mistake... a *big* one.

THE SUITOR. *(With great disappointment)* Mees-take? Ah-h-h-h... no, no.

TONIA. My daughter already got a boyfriend. He's a big shot in the Army.

DOMINIC. *(Enraged, he pounds the table)* MANAGGIA L'AMERICA!

(Tonia picks up the money and begins to hand it back to The Suitor)

DOMINIC. *(Rising)* Whatta you thinka you're doing?

(He grabs part of the money and they struggle over it)

TONIA. *(Smiling)* I say give it back. We don't want it. She's not going to marry him.

DOMINIC. *(Still holding onto the money)* Managgia l'America... and Cristoforo Columbo, too!

THE SUITOR. *(Alarmed)* Signora! Signore! Pleeza!! No fight-a!

(Puts his hands together as if in prayer)

I no wanna make no trouble... I joosta come for a wife-a.

TONIA. *(Nicely)* No trouble at all. But this girl... she is not for you.

SUITOR. *(Tsk-tsk's and shakes his head)* Attsa too bad.

(Hopefully)

You gotta any more daughter?

TONIA. NO! We got no more!

SUITOR. Eh... how... abouta... **niece?**

TONIA. Why don't we look in the goddam phone book!

(The Suitor tips his head to one side and smiles as if that's not a bad idea.)

TONIA. Now, I want you to take your money and go. Back to the farm. It must be time to feed the pigs, no?

(Dominic, still holding the money with his right hand, suddenly clutches his chest with his left hand and bends over)

DOMINIC. A-agh!

TONIA. Oh, my God.

(She lets go of the money)

Look what we are doing. Dominic. Are you all right?

(He is still bent over and silent)

Answer me.

THE SUITOR. *(Frightened)* Signore! Mamma mia.

(Dominic slowly pulls himself up)

DOMINIC. *(He pockets the money)* I'ma all right. I'ma fine.

(To the Suitor)

You. Go down to Del Rio's bar. We talk some more. Alone. **Without women!**

(Angie wails. The Suitor, reassured about Dominic, now is worried about his money)

THE SUITOR. Ma... la moneta*!

DOMINIC. Va. VA. I tole' you, I meet you.

THE SUITOR. *(Petitions the air)* Oh, mamma mia. My money! He's gotta my goddam money!

DOMINIC. *(Shouts and takes a threatening step towards him)* **GO!**

THE SUITOR. *(He screeches as he rushes out in fright)* Jesu! Now he gonna killa me, too! Dey craz-ee is dissa place!

(Outside the screen door, he calls back into them)

You all craz-ee! And you betta bring-a my money, or I call the polizia*!

(He disappears, then quickly re-enters the kitchen)

I'ma no gonna leave without my money!

(Dominic rushes to the drawer and grabs a rolling pin. He chases the suitor our of the kitchen brandishing the rolling pin while they scream at each other in Italian. He returns to the kitchen.)

(The Suitor appears at the outside the window and sticks his head in.)

THE SUITOR. I'ma no gonna leave without my money!

(Dominic rushes again to the door and threatens him loudly. The Suitor finally departs.)

DOMINIC. *(Dominic slams the door)* Allora. Finito.

(He sinks into a chair and pours himself more anisette.)

---

* Mon - A - tah, long "o", long "a" *(money)*
* poL - eh - ZIA *(police)*

(Tonia moves away like a cat. She crosses to Angie and gently steers her to the hallway)

TONIA. *(Quietly)* Get out. Go to your room.

(She puts her fingers to her lips. Angie exits)

(Without changing pace, Tonia crosses to the stove and removes a large pair of pruning shears stored against the wall. She holds them up.)

TONIA. *(Agreeably)* All right. Finito.

(She smiles at Dominic)

Now, if you will excuse me, I have to go out in the backyard and do a little work.

DOMINIC. Eh! What are you gonna do?

TONIA. I'm going to prune the grape vines.

DOMINIC. What are you talkin' about? This is not the time to prune. You will kill the vines.

TONIA. Da vera? No. In my "magica" bones, I feel it is time to prune the vines.

(She slices the air with the shears)

DOMINIC. Non'gia you touch-a my vines!

TONIA. Then give the money back.

DOMINIC. No!

TONIA. He's waiting for you.

DOMINIC. Let him wait. He's justa little stroonz!

TONIA. You better go.

(Cocks her head towards the door and puts a finger behind her ear)

Hear that?

DOMINIC. What? I don't hear nothing.

TONIA. The vines are calling me.

(She makes calling sounds)

"*Tonia... Tonia.*" You don't hear that?

DOMINIC. You're crazy, you know that? Pazzo like a bed bug.

(Tonia slices savagely at the air)

DOMINIC. All right! I'm going. But I'm goin to *talk*. When I get back, if I find-a you touch my vines…

(Makes a threatening gesture with his fist)

… .I gonna breaka you head.

TONIA. Capeesh this one thing, Dominic. You can break my head, and my legs, and even both of my arms. But you can't watch me every minute. If I have to, I will crawl outside on my belly in the middle of the night and *rip* the vines out with my teeth. My daughter is going to marry who she wants.

(Holds up the shears)

So, make up your mind, Dominic DeLuna, give up the money, or give up your vines.

(A long pause. She means business, and Dominic must save face.)

DOMINIC. *(With false humor)* Eh, whatta you get so excited for? Alla you women get too excited for nothing.

(He waves his hand)

I wasn't gonna pick that guy. He's gotta funny eyes, and he's too goddam short.

TONIA. Allora. I respect your very wise decision.

DOMINIC. And whatta am I gonna tell this guy?

TONIA. "Thank you very much, but the famigilia DeLuna, we change our mind." And give him back the money.

(Dominic groans)

Then buy him a beer.

(Dominic groans louder)

Maybe two beers. Maybe a barrel!

DOMINIC. And what am I supposed to use to buy dissa beer?

TONIA. *(Screams at the top of her lungs… her pent up anger)*
USE… YOUR… ZUPPA… ENGLESE… MONEY!

(Stunned, Dominic slinks with his mouth open. Angie, who has been listening at the door, enters.)

ANGIE. Oh, Ma.

TONIA. Come on… come in. It's all over.

(She stashes the shears)

See? You worry for nothing.

ANGIE. Oh, God. He said he had three pigs.

TONIA. You don't have to worry any more about pigs. Never again.

(She puts her arm around her)

Now, tell me. This Victor, he's a nice boy? You like him a lot?

ANGIE. I love him, Ma. But after last night, my life is ruined.

TONIA. Did he call you today?

ANGIE. I don't know. I went to the hospital this morning to sit beside Nonie, and then I went to church. He'll never want to see me again.

TONIA. Not true. How could he not want to see this face, eh?

(She strokes her cheek)

Do you know where this Victor lives?

ANGIE. Yes.

TONIA. Then you go to him now. Tell him that your mother wants to meet him.

ANGIE. What about Papa?

TONIA. We don't have to worry about Papa anymore. No pigs. No Papa.

(Tonia removes bottle and glasses to counter)

Angela, your Papa is old fashioned, yes, but he thinks he does the best for you. He's a good man. And he's worked hard all his life for the family. But he got to make his choice. Now it's time for you to make yours.

ANGIE. I hate him, Ma. But I love him, too. It's crazy.

TONIA. If you think he's bad, you should have seen *my* father. Don't worry. It will pass, and someday, because you are who you are, you will remember only the good things.

(Wipes a crumb from the table with her hand)

Now, promise me one thing with this boy, Angela.

ANGIE. Oh… Ma. You don't have to worry about that. Victor respects me.

TONIA. That's not what I was going to say. I trust you! What I was going to say… if you go with this boy and if you find out that you *don't* love him… don't marry him. Capeesh? You wait. You look til you find the right one.

ANGIE. Ma, you never loved Papa, did you?

TONIA. Eh… love! Angela I want you to listen to me good now because I don't want you to go through what I went through.

(She sits)

I never had a boyfriend. It wasn't allowed. So I never had the chance to find out about myself, what I was like inside. I was told I had a husband waiting for me in America. But that couldn't be so bad because I wouldn't have to live in my father's house anymore.

(Angela begins to interrupt, but Tonia raises her hand to stop her.)

When I was married, I didn't know **anything.** Nobody talked about that stuff. I was never, ever alone with your Papa before the wedding night. It was not allowed. Not even a kiss. On the afternoon of the wedding, my mother told me when I went to bed that night that I should do everything my husband told me. That night, when I went to the dresser and took out a nightgown, your Papa took it away from me.

(She shrugs.)

So I said to myself: "That's all right. I got another one." But he took that one away, too.

(Angela groans)

Aspetto. There's more. The next morning at six o'clock, your Zia Philomena and your Zia Concetta came to the house... **to check the sheets!** They walked right into the bedroom. I was so ashamed it was years before I could look in their faces. And I was **glad** when they both died.

ANGIE. Oh, God... Ma.

TONIA. So..that's what I wanted to say to you.

(Lightening her mood.)

Now, my dolly girl, when you are with this Victor, you hold his hand and you kiss him?

ANGIE. ...yes...

TONIA. It's nice, eh?

ANGIE. Yes.

TONIA. Good!!

(She removes the sugar bowl from shelf and sets it on the table)

TONIA. I'm going to give you some money, cara. You take Victor to Pippie's for some pizza, or something, si? And then bring him back here and I will meet him after Rocco brings me from the hospital.

(She hasn't removed the cover of the bowl)

ANGIE. *(Puts her hand over Tonia's to stop her)* I have money, Ma. I got paid yesterday. Besides, Victor wouldn't let me pay. He's like that.

TONIA. All right, cara.

(She returns the bowl to the shelf)

ANGIE. Mamma... thank you.

TONIA. No, my dolly girl. I thank you. I always knew I was going to tell you all this but I never knew how. It feels so good that we will never have to worry about it anymore. Never again.

ANGIE. I love you, Ma.

(They hug and hold each other in an embrace while the lights come down to black.)

End Act II – Scene II

Scene III

(Several hours later. When the lights come up, Sonny is talking on the telephone. He has just put on a clean shirt and is buttoning up the last buttons as he speaks. His lunch box is on the counter. In the distance, the sound of a siren can be faintly heard. He paces as he speaks.)

SONNY. Listen to me. Carlo! Don't hang up. I know I still owe you a few bucks but this time I promise... with interest.

(He listens)

There's no one else I can go to. Please.

(He hedges)

A few thousand. That's all. Three. It was something I had to do. It was a big game and the stakes were... I mean, I *almost* had it.

Carlo? Carlo? Don't... oh... dammit. *Dammit.*

(He slams the receiver down and curses at the telephone)

Favote! Who the hell needs you.

(Angrily, he crosses towards his bedroom. As he gets past the refrigerator, Maria La Brutta can be seen tip-toeing stealthily up to peer into the screen door. Sonny sees that someone is outside and he flattens himself against the refrigerator. At this sudden move, Maria jumps back out of sight)

SONNY. Someone is out there. Who is it?
MARIA. *(Peeks around the corner)* Is that you, Sonny DeLuna?
SONNY. Who wants to know?
MARIA. Maria. Maria Frascella.
SONNY. Who?
MARIA. *(In full view, she tries to open the door but it is hooked shut)* Just take a look and see who it is, for Chris-sake. And open this door. I can't stand out here all day.
SONNY. Maria. What do you want. What are you doing here?

(He unlatches the door and lets her in)

MARIA. Are you alone?

SONNY. Yeah, I'm alone.

(A siren can be softly heard in the distance)

MARIA. Is there another way out? In case your mother comes home?

SONNY. Through the hallway and out the front door. Why? What's my mother going to do to you?

MARIA. Niente. Just break my back, that's all.

SONNY. What?

MARIA. Shut up and listen. You know, I shouldn't be here. I am sticking my neck out for you.

SONNY. I don't know what you're talking about!

MARIA. I said... *shut up and listen.* I gotta talk fast.

(Pulls out a chair and sits at the table.)

Allora. I was at a private party last night. In the south end. A nice place off of Franklin Avenue.

SONNY. Yeah?

MARIA. There were a lot of people there.

SONNY. So, what's that to me?

MARIA. If you will just let me tell you! Do you know a man they call "Cappello"... .because he wears that funny hat all the time? I mean, he wears it *all* the time.

(The sirens are more persistent)

SONNY. What about him?

MARIA. He is always with another guy they call Nino. Do you know these men?

SONNY. I know 'em. What do you want to know for?

MARIA. This "Cappello" doesn't say too much. He just sits back and watches everything, with that hat pushed way over his eyes.

(A beat)

They stare, those eyes, like the snake waiting to jump

on the mouse. One minute the mouse is fine, eating his piece of provolone and minding his own goddam business and the next he is swallowed up whole. Teeth, tail e tutti cosi.

(She gestures with her six-fingered glove)

And that Nino! I think the smell of blood is like perfume to him. Capeesh? Well, he had a few too many bicchieri. So he let slip out a few things.

(Brings her hand up to her mouth to indicate drinking)

This was all later. After everyone left. You know?

SONNY. So what?

MARIA. Sonny, have you been running numbers with these men. Or what?

SONNY. No numbers.

MARIA. It's bigger?

(He doesn't answer. She angers)

Sonny, please. I shouldn't even be here. If they find out… for Chris-sake. Answer me.

SONNY. How do I know they didn't send you?

MARIA. I never get mixed up with that kind of stuff. I stay clear. I got to worry for myself in this city… capeesh? You know me from hanging around DePasquale's.

SONNY. Yeah. So?

MARIA. I didn't pay too much attention to them at first. They don't live in this city so I thought they were talking about another place, some other man. But then they started to say "Donato this," and "Donato that… " and then I hear… "Donato DeLuna… the *cripple.*"

SONNY. And… .what did they say about… Donato… "the *cripple.*"

MARIA. They said you stole money. Da vera?

(Sirens in background come closer)

SONNY. I didn't steal nothin'. I just borrowed it. They're gonna get every penny back as soon as I can…

acquire... it.

MARIA. They said you been taking a little here... a little there... for a long time now. Non capisco, Sonny. What is your involvement?

SONNY. The cops were gettin' wise so they let me and two other guys take turns carryin' the pay-off money. That's all. No big deal.

MARIA. Ah! They said they knew one of you was taking money. So where is it? Where's the money?

SONNY. Last night I got in the biggest game of my life. I was winnin'... right up to the last hand. I would've had enough to help Ma out. We could leave my grandmother in St. Francis instead of putting her in the state hospital next week. And I saw this diamond ring in the window at Savitt's, perfect for Marilyn. She would have come crawlin' back. I know it. When she saw that ring, she'd know I was somebody.

(He paces)

And I could have sneaked the money back to them and they never would have known the difference.

MARIA. Eh, Sonny, please! What's the matter with you! They know where every penny is. Capeesh? How could you let it happen?

SONNY. It was so easy! This jerk I'm taking money from all night... like taking candy off a baby... ..he wins it all in the last hand and walks out the door.

(He stops)

I never saw him before in my life and he walks out the door with my guts in his pocket.

MARIA. So you borrowed the money and lost.

(Another siren goes past the house)

SONNY. A few thousand is nothin' to them. They throw it around like water. And they never would have known it. It was gonna be the last time, I swear.

MARIA. Sonny, the whole thing was a set-up.

(Sonny begins to react, but another very loud siren distracts him. He hurries to the door and looks out)

SONNY. What the hell is going' on? There must be *some* fire someplace.

MARIA. Eh… there's a fire at the circus, or something. I heard it on the radio.

(Sonny rushes to the radio and turns it on. He gets static)

MARIA. Shut the radio off! At a time like this, he puts on the radio. Forget the dam fire engines and listen to me!

(Before he finds the news station, he gets static and music combined)

Come on. Shut if off. I'm talking to you.

SONNY. *Shut… up!*

RADIO ANNOUNCER. A FIRE BROKE OUT DURING THIS AFTERNOON'S MATINEE PERFORMANCE AT THE RINGLING-BROTHERS-BARNUM AND BAILEY CIRCUS ON THE BARBOUR STREET FAIRGROUNDS. THERE HAVE BEEN FATALITIES.

IN JUST A FEW MINUTES, WE WILL TURN YOU OVER TO GEORGE BOWE AND BERNARD MULLINS WHO WERE AT THE SCENE OF THE FIRE MINUTES AFTER IT BROKE OUT, BUT WHO ARE NOW AT THE STATE ARMORY IN HARTFORD WHERE A TEMPORARY MORGUE HAS BEEN SET UP.

(Sonny turns down the volume)

SONNY. A temporary morgue!? Oh, my God… oh, my God. Nicky!!

ANNOUNCER. STAY TUNED TO THIS STATION AND WE WILL INTERRUPT WITH FURTHER BULLETINS ON THE CIRCUS FIRE.

(Music)

(The telephone rings. Sonny starts to rush toward it)

MARIA. DON'T ANSWER IT!

SONNY. I gotta answer it. You don't understand. Maybe it's Nicky.

MARIA. *(Crosses to radio and turns it off)* It might be **them,** Sonny.

(The phone continues to ring. Sonny starts for the phone once more. Maria holds the receiver in its cradle and they struggle over it)

MARIA. *(Screaming at him)* YOU don't understand. They got **revolvers!**

(Sonny stops. With trepidation, Maria raises her hand to indicate that she will answer the phone. She swallows, picks up the receiver and places her hand over the mouthpiece)

Pronto. *(Controlled, she listens)* La casa DeLuna... si.

(She listens her face reflecting her fear. She replaces the receiver in a daze)

You gotta get out of here. Now!

SONNY. Who was it?

MARIA. If it's who I *think* it is... God forbid! He said... you got thirty minutes head start and then you are "carne di cane.*" Dog meat. You gotta get out. Now.

SONNY. I just can't go... I can't.

MARIA. GO!

SONNY. *(Desperate; crying)* Where? Where am I going to go? Where am I going to go, Maria!

MARIA. Someplace. Anyplace! Where you can hide out until you figure out what to do.

SONNY. I don't have any money to go anyplace.

MARIA. *(Takes wallet out her purse and quickly removes some bills)* Here's fifty dollars. All I got on me. Take it.

SONNY. No. No.

MARIA. God damn it. Take it.

(She shoves the money at him)

---

* *karn dee KAHN*

I gotta get out of here myself.

(She crosses to the door and stops)

Per carita*, Sonny. You got less than thirty minutes. Go. And don't look back.

SONNY. Maria! Thanks.

MARIA. Eh.

(She crosses to him and hugs him.)

Sonny, you were the only kid who ever said hello me. Ciao.

(She exits hurriedly)

(Panicked, Sonny rushes to the counter and picks up his car keys. He grabs a jacket off the couch and feels for money in the pockets. There is none. He hurls the jacket aside. He opens the kitchen drawer and rummages around for change, then slams it shut when finds there is none. He picks up the piggy-bank and dumps the few coins into his hand. He throws them aside in frustration.)

(He remembers! He looks at the sugar bowl, approaches it slowly and stands in front of it. He stares at it. Then he carefully carries it to the table, lifts off the lid and stares at the wad of bills. He struggles with himself and begins to put the lid back, but the sound of a car horn outside startles him. He removes the lid again and this time he scoops up the bills and shoves them into his pocket. He replace the lid, and returns the sugar bowl to its rightful place on the shelf. He exits out the front door hallway in a hurry.)

End Act II – Scene III

---

* *karr-ee-TAH (for pity's sake)*

Scene IV

(Several hours later. The lights come up on an empty kitchen. Rocco hurries onto the porch and knocks at the screen door.)

(Tonia enters from the bedroom hall.)

TONIA. Rocco. What is the matter with you? I tell you not to come back anymore and you keep showing up! You got a rope tied from your leg to this house?

ROCCO. Tonia, don't be mad. I just saw Angie at Pippie's. She introduced me to her boyfriend. A soldier.

(Tonia relents.)

TONIA. All right. Come in.

(She removes her apron.)

Tell me about this... Victor.

ROCCO. He seemed like a fine young man, Tonia. He stood up when he shook my hand. A nice, strong handshake. And it don't hurt that's he Italian, either.

TONIA. So. What did Angie say?

ROCCO. She was so happy. She said, "Rocco. This is my *innamorato**.

(Smiling after her)

Innamorato. What a beautiful word.

(He pronounces it slowly and trills the "r")

In-nam-o-r-r-r-ato. Che bella musica*... no?

TONIA. Eh. It's just a word. That's all.

ROCCO. A man could wait forever if he knew a love like that is returned.

TONIA. If he waits too long, he could die of old age, too.

ROCCO. Maybe he chooses to live alone rather than to compromise his dream.

(Tonia studies his face. Takes a deep breath and several beats while she considers a momentous decision.)

---

* *in - nam - o - ROT - o (lover)*
* *moo - si - ca*

TONIA. I have to try something. I need your help.

ROCCO. Sure.

(Tonia pulls two chairs down side-by-side in front of the table. She sits in one, and pats the other chair once firmly)

TONIA. Sit.

(Puzzled, Rocco does as she instructs. Tonia thrusts her arm out straight at him.)

Hold my hand.

(He looks at her in surprise)

Hold my hand!

(Rocco takes her hand, but he's not sure just how to hold it.)

TONIA. I said… hold my hand.

(He gets her hand in a natural position and they sit quietly while he holds her hand. Tonia is trying to fathom her feelings during this encounter and we see her listening to her inner emotions)

TONIA. *(Nods)* All right.

(She turns to Rocco)

Now, do you think you could try to kiss me?

(Rocco's eyes bug out. He cannot believe his great good luck, and he can hardly contain himself. He plants his feet on the floor, turns her chin toward him and very gently and tenderly kisses her mouth in a brief kiss. He draws back to study her. Tonia's brows knit as she analyzes the kiss. Again, she nods)

(Next, Rocco takes her to him again and begins the second kiss as tenderly. Tonia cooperates. But he becomes increasingly more ardent and his passionate kiss become so over-whelmingly wild, Tonia starts to pull away, protesting loudly while his mouth is still glued to hers. She manages to get away with one violent wrench. Rocco falls across the chairs and to the floor when she gets away.)

TONIA. *(Furious)* That is too much, goddam it! Sporaccacione*!!

(She punches him in the shoulder)

ROCCO. Tonia, I am sorry. I am sorry.

(He pulls himself together)

What is a man supposed to do?

TONIA. *(Trembling from the experience)* God forgive me.

(She wants him, but is terrified at it.)

What happened just now... I am not a puttana.

ROCCO. Madonna mia! How could I think such a terrible thing?

TONIA. All right. Thank you very much, but I think you better go now and don't come back any more.

ROCCO. Thank you very much?

(He's stunned)

Thank you very much?! That's it? I have to go?

TONIA. It's best.

ROCCO. Best? Best for *who?*

TONIA. All right. Then promise me that next time you will go slower.

ROCCO. Next time?

(Ecstatic, he beseeches the statue.)

Did you hear that, St. Anthony?? She said **next time!**

TONIA. But you better watch out. I'm no puttana. It might be years and we both might be dead. Now go!

(Picks up his jacket and hat and crosses to the door. The telephone rings. Tonia picks it up)

Hello.

(She listens)

Five minutes. What is that?

(She shrugs)

Five minutes? Hello? Hello?

---

* spork - ah - CHONE *(Filthy fellow)*

(She holds the receiver out and looks at it in bewilderment, and hangs up.)

Something is very wrong. That was not a kid. That was a man.

(She looks at the clock.)

It's five o'clock. I know where everybody is. Dominic's at DelRio's, Angela went to Victor's, and Nicky went to the circus. The only one I didn't see is Sonny.

ROCCO. Tonia. Nicky went to the circus?

(He crosses to her)

Did you say that Nicky went to the *circus?*

TONIA. Why? What's wrong?

(The panic begins)

You know something. Rocco! What's the matter?

ROCCO. Is there any chance he could have gone someplace else?

TONIA. No. He went to the circus with John Malucci.

ROCCO. Now, don't get excited. We don't know anything for sure yet.

TONIA. *(She pounds at his chest, but he grabs her arms)* Will you ***please*** tell me!)

ROCCO. *(Tries to speak calmly)* There was a fire today at the circus. I heard it on the radio. But we don't know for sure if Nicky went there.

TONIA. That was the smoke we saw from the bus. Oh, my God. Rocco! There were fire engines and ambulances all over the streets.

(She begins to sob)

Oh, my God! Please don't let anything happen to my Nicky. Sant'Antonio mio, let my Nicky be all right. Please, Rocco, you gotta take me there.

ROCCO. No. Wait a minute. Let me think.

TONIA. There's nothing to think about.

ROCCO. *(Crosses to radio and turns it on. Static)* They won't let us through. Aspetto. Calm down.

ANNOUNCER. EYE WITNESSES INSIDE THE TENT SAID THAT ANIMAL CAGES BLOCKED SOME OF THE AISLES AND MANY MET THEIR DEATHS BY BEING TRAMPLED UNDERFOOT IN THE PANIC AS THE CANVAS EXPLODED IN SMOKE AND FLAMES.

TONIA. *(She screams)* NICKY!

(Dominic enters. Stops when he sees the scenario.)

DOMINIC. Tonia, it's true? At the bar, they say there's a fire where Nicky go. My, God! How can there be a fire at the circus?

(He begins to choke up)

ANNOUNCER. RELATIVES ARE REQUESTED TO STAY OUT THE AREA. WE'LL BE SWITCHING OVER TO THE STATE ARMORY ON BROAD STREET SHORTLY WHERE A TEMPORARY MORGUE…

(Rocco turns the radio off.)

DOMINIC. Jesu, Guiseppe, Maria. I gotta go there, Tonia. Rocco, we gotta find Nicky. You take-a me?

ROCCO. No, Compare. I go. My car is right outside. We got a better chance if I go myself. Capeeesh? You got to stay here in case Nicky try to call on the phone. Promise me you both stay!

DOMINIC. All right. All right. We stay. But Compare, ***per l'amore di Dio, va subito*! Subito!*** Go fast… fast!

ROCCO. I go fast as I can.

(Rocco exits in a rush. Dominic turns the radio on)

TONIA. Dominic… .

(She reaches out to him.)

ANNOUNCER. WE ARE REPORTING TO YOU FROM THE STATE ARMORY. THE ANIMAL ACTS WERE OVER AND THE FLYING WALENDAS HAD JUST TAKEN THEIR PLACES ON THE HIGH WIRE WHEN THE FIRE ERUPTED IN THE CANVAS WITHIN SECONDS. NOW THE GRIM TASK OF IDENTIFYING

---

* *SOO - bee - to, with a long "o" on "to" (hurry)*

THE BODIES NOW FACES HYSTERICAL RELATIVES LINING THE STREET.

(Tonia screams. Dominic struggles to remain calm as he turns off the radio)

DOMINIC. *(He turns to the Statue of St. Anthony. He blesses himself. Quietly, he puts his hands together and beseeches.)*
Dear God... Sant'Antonio, please. If you let our Nicky be all right, from the bottom of my heart... for the rest of my life-a... I promise you...

(Dominic covers his face with his hands and makes his pledge silently. Suddenly, Sonny enters the kitchen from the front hallway. He leads Nicky into the kitchen. Nicky is crying, his face dirty and clothes torn and smoke-stained. He runs to his mother.)

DOMINIC. Tonia... Tonia. Look.

(She looks up and leaps to her feet.)

Look who's here.

TONIA. Oh, thank you, God. Thank you, St. Anthony... for giving us back our son.

(Dominic places a kiss on the foot of the statue.)

SONNY. He's okay, Ma. See? He's just a little dirty. So is John Malucci. They're all right. I found them wandering around in a daze after they jumped from the bleachers and crawled under the tent. Besides, I wouldn't let anything happen to ole' chooch, here.

(Tonia covers Nicky's face with kisses)

TONIA. Please, Dominic... help me to wash him up and put him to bed.

DOMINIC. Come-on... come-on, figlio... you home now with Mama and PaPa. We go easy... easy.

(Dominic leads Nicky out. Tonia trails behind.)

SONNY. Ma, you know I would have never let anything happen to him. You *do* know that, don't you?

TONIA. *(At door, she stops, and returns to Sonny and kisses him* *tenderly on the cheek. She holds his hands and looks deeply into his eyes.)*

Thank you... my son.

(She exits quietly)

(Sonny sidles backwards to the cupboard shelf, keeping his eyes on the door to the hallway. He turns quickly and takes down the sugar bowl. He sets it on the table facing the audience but is so intent on replacing the wad of bills, he does not see Nino come up on the porch. He clamps the lid on the sugar bowl and returns it to its usual place on the shelf. Nino stands at the screen door, and sees that Sonny is alone. He opens the screen door a crack, steps partially in, aims a gun at Sonny and calls quietly.)

NINO. *(smiling)* Hey. DeLuna.

(Sonny turns and sees Nino and begins to back away. At the same moment. Dominic enters. He is between Sonny and Nino. When he sees the gun pointed at Sonny, he shouts and rushes at Nino.)

SONNY. No! Pa..no!

Blackout

(A shot is heard in the blackout)

End of Scene IV

Scene V
(The family united)

In this final scene, there is no dialogue. Before the lights come up, poignant and moving music is heard softly and underscores the entire action of the scene.

It is four days later, early morning, as the family is preparing to go to Dominic's funeral.

When the lights come up, Victor is knocking at the door. Angie enters, dressed in an appropriate black dress, and crosses to the door to let him in. He hugs her, consoling her as she has been weeping. Angie crosses to the daybed and sits. Victor trails behind her.

A very sad and woe-begone Nicky enters from the bedroom. He is wearing black trousers and a short-sleeved white shirt, which is partially tucked in. He crosses to Angie who helps him tuck in the shirt-tail. She pulls him down beside her on the couch and encircles him in a comforting embrace.

Tonia enters from the bedroom, dressed in a black dress. When she enters, Victor rises. Tonia is carrying Sonny's black jacket, as well as her hat. She hangs the jacket on the back of a chair as she goes to the mirror on puts on her hat.

Rocco, dressed in a black suit, comes to the back door. He is there to escort them to church.

Sonny enters in black trousers and white shirt. Tonia holds his jacket out and he slips into it, but he struggles with his necktie. Victor crosses to Sonny and reaches out. He adjusts his tie and pats it in place. Sonny nods his thanks and they hug in acceptance of each other.

Rocco holds the door open for Victor, Angie and Nicky as they exit the kitchen Rocco follows them.

Tonia and Sonny are alone. They face each other. With great inner strength, Tonia holds her arms out to Sonny and he goes to her, lays his head on her shoulder and weeps. Tonia strokes his face and kisses his cheek as she forgives him. She straightens his jacket, smooths his hair back, and nods that they are ready.

Rocco returns to the door, holds it open for Tonia and Sonny. They exit. Rocco is alone and he slowly closes the kitchen door as the lights come down and out.

THE END

PROPERTY LIST

Pre-set Properties
Notebook and pencil on table
Coffee cup on table
Coffee pot on stove
Fan on top of refrigerator
Bowl brush on rocking chair
Broom in corner
Glass cookie jar with biscotti
Dishes, silverware
Glasses of various sizes
Two extra large water glasses
Large butcher knife in drawer
Pay envelope on shelf
Medicine bottle with pills
Small bag with candy
Half-gallon jug of red wine
Statue of St. Anthony
Pruning shears
Sugar bowl with lid
Loaf bread, opt.
Bottle of Anisette
Dish towels, cloth
Colander
Nicky's sandals
Sonny's roll of bills

Furniture List
Stove
Refrigerator
Sink; counter with drawer
Kitchen table, chairs
Rocking chair
Cushion for rocking chair
Telephone table
Black dial telephone
Clock
Daybed with coverlet
Open shelves for dishes
Shelf for St. Anthony statue
Mirror on wall
Standing coat rack (with apron)

In Refrigerator
Roll of salami
One bottle of beer
Bowl with macaroni salad

Lighting Fixtures
Simple hanging light over the kitchen table
Light switch inside back door

Sound Effects
Radio announcements
   (1) War bulletins, etc..
   (2) Circus promo, circus music
Fire sirens

Alley Scene
Metal trash barrel

Property Table (Off)
(Act I)
Angie – Shoe box
Tonia – Large tote bag with thermos
Sonny – Metal lunch box
Dominic – Bunch of greens from garden
Personal Props
Nicky – note book & pencil
Tonia – dollar bill
Angie – prayer book, lace head scarf
Nino – cigarette, revolver

Property Table (Off)
(Act II)
Dominic – metal lunch box

Personal Props
Nicky – note book & pencil
Tonia – dollar bill
Angie – prayer book, lace head scarf
Nino – cigarette, revolver
Maria – white gloves, one glove with six fingers
Victor – rolled up newspaper
Sonny – two tickets to circus
Suitor – large wad of bills

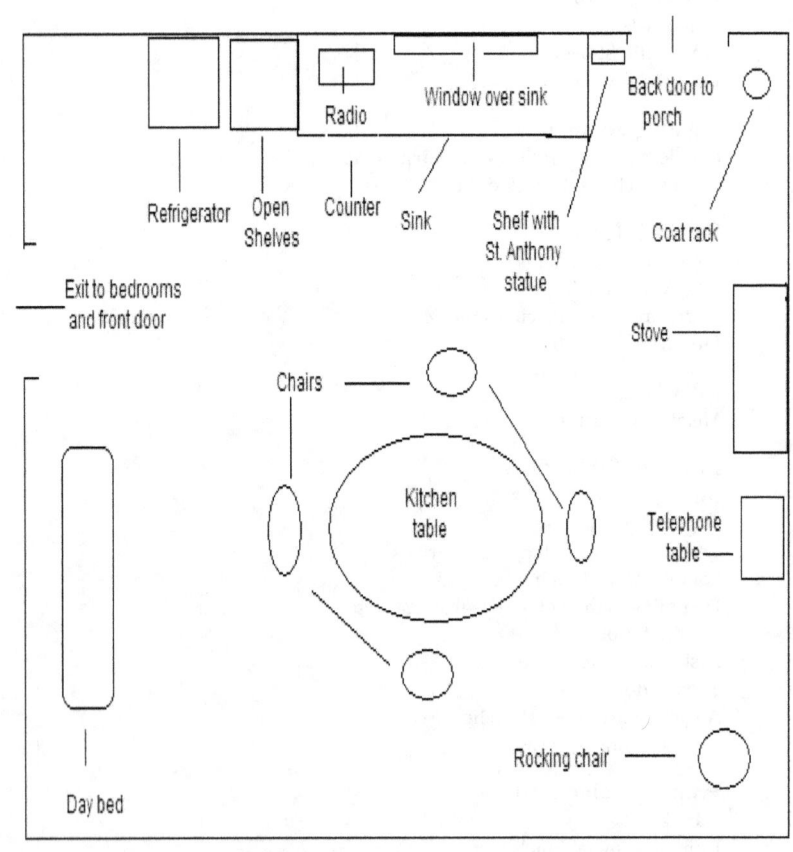

FRONT STREET SET

**Also by
Anne Pié...**

At First Sight

Wild Mushrooms

Please visit our website **samuelfrench.com** for complete
descriptions and licensing information

From the Reviews of
FRONT STREET...

"Powerful, ethnic family drama, circa 1944, written with passion and a strong sense of family ties... characters strong, volatile and dynamically developed."
- Pat Taylor, *Tolucan Times*

"GET A FRONT SEAT FOR FRONT STREET. *Front Street* is a delightful slice of Italian-American brought to life by a smartly written script depicting the struggle between Old World tradition and the strange new one."
- Dean Edward, NOHO- LA

"It sometimes is sad that there aren't more well-made plays around today like *Front Street*. It's enjoyable and fulfilling. They argue no political agent and current events are generally left to news broadcasts. Character and relationships are at the core of the genre."
- T. H. McCulloh, *Online Entertainment*

"Like *Death of a Salesman*, Anne Pié's *Front Street* has a larger-than-life feel. It's a delight for eye, ear, heart, mind. In her tale of an Italian immigrant family living in Hartford in 1944, the play achieves a near mythic quality."
- Su Harrington, *Erie Times-News*

"*Front Street* season's best at Seven Angels. Anne Pié's *Front Street* is the playwright's tip of the hat to old-world Italian families, their strong ties, loony religious beliefs and heated arguments around the kitchen table."
- James V. Ruocco, *Republican American*

"What is so apparent in the writing is the realistic nature of the characters and the developments of the sometimes comic and tragic events that transpire. The story never falters. A paean of praise should be sung to Mrs. Pié."
- Edgar Kloten, *The Hartford Courant*

"Once in a lifetime, twice if one is lucky, a buff of repertory theater gets to see a play so overpowering that the histrionics of regular theater are forgotten and a thrust of reality takes over. With *Front Street* it's as if a fourth wall of a tenement has been removed and we are allowed to look in on the actual life of an Italian family some 60 years ago.
- Bob Harrington, *West Hartford, Theater Review*

"*Front Street* is a genuine cultural phenomenon, recalling memories of a time, a mood, a people who played a vital role in the state's history."
- Henry M. Keezing, *The Herald*

OTHER TITLES AVAILABLE FROM SAMUEL FRENCH

JACK GOES BOATING
Bob Glaudini

Full Length / Comedy / 2m, 2f / Interior
Four flawed but likeable lower-middle-class New Yorkers interact in a touching and warmhearted play about learning how to stay afloat in the deep water of day-to-day living. Laced with cooking classes, swimming lessons and a smorgasbord of illegal drugs, *Jack Goes Boating* is a story of date panic, marital meltdown, betrayal, and the prevailing grace of the human spirit.

"An immensely likable play [that] exudes a wry compassion."
- *The New York Times*

"Endearing romantic comedy about a married couple and the social-misfit friends they fix up. Witty and knowing and all heart."
- *Variety*

"Glides effortlessly from the shallow end of the emotional pool to the deep end."
- *Theatremania.com*

SAMUELFRENCH.COM

www.ingramcontent.com/pod-product-compliance
Lightning Source LLC
Chambersburg PA
CBHW070645300426
44111CB00013B/2272